DE PROPRIETATIBUS LITTERARUM

*edenda curat*

C. H. VAN SCHOONEVELD

*Indiana University*

*Series Maior, 26*

# SINGLE NATURE'S DOUBLE NAME

## The Collectedness of the Conflicting in British and American Romanticism

*by*

RAYMOND BENOIT

1973

MOUTON

THE HAGUE · PARIS

LIBRARY OF CONGRESS CATALOG CARD NUMBER 73-81272

Printed in The Netherlands by ZND, Den Bosch

*What appeals most to each reader is dedicated to my wife Sharon, to my mother and father, and to my brothers William and Robert.*

Single nature's double name
Neither two nor one was called.

Reason, in itself confounded,
Saw division grow together,
To themselves yet either neither;
Simple were so well compounded

That it cried, "How true a twain
Seemeth this concordant one!"

"The Phoenix and the Turtle"

William Shakespeare

# ACKNOWLEDGEMENTS

A number of sections in this book are revisions of essays published in periodicals. I am grateful to the editors of the following journals for kindly allowing me to use the material: *American Literature*, "Emerson on Plato: the Fire's Center", 34 (1963), 487-498, and "Walden as God's Drop", 43 (1971), 122-124; *Bucknell Review*, "Theology and Literature: *The Scarlet Letter*", XX (1972), 83-92; *Costerus*, "In Dear Detail by Ideal Light: 'Ode on a Grecian Urn'", 3 (1972); *Thought*, "The New American Poetry", XLIV (1969), 201-218; *Walt Whitman Review*, "The Mind's Return: Whitman, Teilhard, and Jung", XIII (1967), 21-28. I am also grateful to Mr. Howard Nemerov for permission to quote "Runes XV" and "Trees" from *New & Selected Poems* (Chicago: University of Chicago Press, 1963); and to Harper & Row for "Representing Far Places" from *Traveling through the Dark* (New York, 1962) by William Stafford.

# CONTENTS

# PART ONE

I

# COLERIDGE: THE PHILOSOPHY OF ROMANTICISM

> But you forget that the matter of which I speak is, in all
> respects, the very "mind" or "spirit" of the schools, so far
> as regards its high capacities, and is, moreover, the
> "matter" of these schools at the same time. God, with all
> the powers attributed to spirit, is but the perfection of
> matter.
>
> Edgar Allan Poe

1

Coleridge's theory of the imagination is the most important ramification of his philosophy and the most influential aesthetic doctrine to emerge from the Romantic movement. The heart of the theory, balance as well as reconciliation, was to the nineteenth century what felt thought has become to the twentieth. The logical separation between the material and the spiritual was the overriding concern of nineteenth century writers. They reacted to it symbolically: in the symbol, or *Sinnbild*, the division between meaning and image is overcome while the difference between both is maintained. The symbol as the poem is one reality but it encompasses mind and matter. In doing so, it accepts and fulfills the contrary and simultaneous drives of human nature towards "succession of time and unmoving eternity, infinite change and ineffable rest".[1] An example of this is the last stanza of Keats's "Ode to Psyche" where what begins as mind passes unnoticeably into world while we nevertheless remember that we are still in mind. What begins as metaphor gradually becomes fact too, which then is returned intact to metaphor to begin all over again. In this way the poem as the symbolic work continually coaxes away the division between the indivisibility of the mind and the divisibility of the world while their difference is maintained:

[1] Samuel Taylor Coleridge, *The Complete Works*, ed. W. G. T. Shedd (New York, 1864), IV, 42.

Yes, I will be thy priest, and build a fane
In some untrodden region of my mind,
Where branched thoughts, new grown with pleasant pain,
Instead of pines shall murmur in the wind:
Far, far around shall those dark-cluster'd trees
Fledge the wild-ridged mountains steep by steep;
And there by zephyrs, streams, and birds, and bees,
The moss-lain Dryads shall be lull'd to sleep;
And in the midst of this wide quietness
A rosy sanctuary will I dress
With the wreath'd trellis of a working brain,
With buds, and bells, and stars without a name...

Wordsworth's doctrine of memory is similar for he also desires to give
time a permanent abode:

> when thy mind
> Shall be a mansion for all lovely forms,
> Thy memory be as a dwelling place
> For all sweet sounds and harmonies...                    ("Tintern Abbey")

In his poem "Vermeer", the contemporary poet Howard Nemerov states
this desire of the Romantic poet crisply and directly:

If I could say to you, and make it stick,
A girl in a red hat, a woman in blue
Reading a letter, a lady weighing gold...
If I could say this to you so you saw...[2]

The idea is not to replace saying with seeing, for we would no more be
robbed of Nemerov's words than Vermeer's paint: paint and the word
establish the human response and seal it to the world to create the
symbolic continuum. The poet would have his word be his word but a
deed as well: If I could say this to you so you saw. D. H. Lawrence, who
came to this again and again himself, dramatizes the issue and the reaction
in this exchange from *Women in Love* about Birkin's statements and
restatements about the paradise of infinite change and ineffable rest:

"I can't make out – neither can he nor anybody. He seems to think that if
you marry you can get through marriage into a third heaven, or something –
all very vague."...

"He says," she added, with a grimace of irony, "that you can find an eternal
equilibrium in marriage, if you accept the unison, and still leave yourself
separate, don't try to fuse."...

"Le paradis!" mocked Gudrun.[3]

---

[2] *The Next Room of the Dream* (Chicago, 1962), 37.
[3] New York, 1963, 282-283.

In many ways all this begins with Coleridge "who anticipated in many important respects", Herbert Read remarked, "the point of view to which the philosophy of our own time is busily returning".[4] It is busily returning to his view of the imagination as the symbol-making faculty because the problem of disjunction in all its forms is so much our own. Coleridge knew that man "reveals reality to himself, and himself to reality", in the words of Ernst Cassirer, "in that he lets himself and the environment enter into this plastic medium, in which the two do not merely make contact, but fuse with each other".[5] The imagination heals the gaping wound between mind and things. For Coleridge it is the medium where man and nature perpetuate their higher reunion – consciousness and the objects of consciousness (the world as the unconscious) – after the development of self-awareness itself has first alienated man from the world around him and then turned man back to that world in turning upon himself as the object (unconscious) of his own thought. The "mystery of genius in the Fine Arts" is defined accordingly: "to make the external internal, the internal external, to make nature thought, and thought nature..."[6]

Theorists of modern poetry and other arts do indeed return to Coleridge but the debt is often either unacknowledged or denied, sometimes vehemently, altogether. Murray Krieger has written in *The New Apologists for Poetry* that "if we follow down the line that starts with Hulme. we find the same seemingly contradictory duality...: an uncompromising prejudice against romanticism coupled with an invocation of romantic and Coleridgean concepts, even when Coleridge has been slandered by name"; "this concept of imagination [some] explicitly reject even as they smuggle it into their theory".[7] In chapter fourteen of the *Biographia Literaria* Coleridge defined his idea of the imagination:

The poet, described in *ideal* perfection, brings the whole soul of man into activity, with the subordination of its faculties to each other, according to their relative worth and dignity. He diffuses a tone and spirit of unity, that blends, and (as it were) *fuses*, each into each, by that synthetic and magical power, to which we have exclusively appropriated the name of imagination. This power, first put in action by the will and understanding, and retained under their irremissive, though gentle and unnoticed, controul... reveals itself in the balance or reconciliation of opposite or discordant qualities: of sameness, with

---

[4] *The True Voice of Feeling* (New York, 1953), 173.
[5] *Language and Myth*, trans. Susanne K. Langer (New York, 1953), 10.
[6] Samuel Taylor Coleridge, *Biographia Literaria*, ed. J. Shawcross (London, 1958), II, 258. Hereafter all page references are in the text.
[7] Minneapolis, 1956, 35.

difference; of the general, with the concrete; the idea, with the image; the individual, with the representative; the sense of novelty and freshness, with old and familiar objects; a more than usual state of emotion, with more than usual order; judgement ever awake and steady self-possession, with enthusiasm and feeling profound or vehement; and while it blends and harmonizes the natural and the artificial, still subordinates art to nature; the manner to the matter; and our admiration of the poet to our sympathy with the poetry. (II, 12)

If we can understand this theory, we will understand the basis of Romanticism for, as Mr. Krieger continues, "in their battle against romanticism some of the most influential of modern critics have set themselves against the completely romantic Coleridgean imagination".[8] Still the concept continually reappears in individual terminology. It is not difficult to see how the "balance or reconciliation of opposite or discordant qualities" looms in the background of the New Criticism. Yvor Winters and Allen Tate, for instance, judge a poem according to the unity of the furthest extremes of denotation and connotation, of extension and intension. For Cleanth Brooks and Robert Penn Warren the standard is wit, paradox, or irony – i.e., a balance of opposite or discordant qualities. As Warren wrote, "the poet wishes to indicate that his vision has been earned, that it can survive reference to the complexities and contradictions of experience. And irony is one such device of reference."[9] Such readings of Coleridge – acknowledged or denied – have indeed made criticism a very sophisticated exercise. Coleridge, however, had more than literary irony in mind when he defined the imagination. He had a whole philosophy in mind which was distinctly theological in its orientation: "philosophy directed the course and determined the ends of Coleridge's criticism."[10] We have a triple reduction: to understand Romanticism it is necessary to understand the theory of the imagination, and understanding that depends upon understanding the philosophy it was built upon. After this, the poetry itself falls into perspective because "the theory, at least in some phases, seems to have in mind a kind of poetry which will somehow... be the appointed representative of the basic philosophy".[11] Furthermore, "Romantic poems tend to be about romantic imagination."[12]

[8]   *The New Apologists for Poetry*, 32.
[9]   *Selected Essays* (New York, 1958), 29.
[10]  Herbert Read, *The True Voice of Feeling*, 181.
[11]  William Wimsatt and Cleanth Brooks, *Literary Criticism: A Short History* (New York, 1957), 399.
[12]  Wimsatt and Brooks, 404.

2

The philosophy out of which this theory of the imagination developed
was German philosophy, particularly that of Friedrich Schelling, and it
involved a "revolution of thought such as only occurs once or twice in a
millennium".[13] That revolution was the redirection of the mind towards
looking at things in a dipolar way, from God's own nature on down in a
series of unified antitheses based archetypally on the first divine synthesis:
man and God, conscious and unconscious, man and nature, subject and
object; and including a series of related antitheses: matter and spirit,
time and eternity, finitude and infinitude, reality and ideality. The
revolution was away from monopolarity towards dipolarity. That is,
the Romantic writers and the Romantic philosophers brought all those
things back that had been exiled by the neoclassic writers and the philosophers of the Enlightenment. Their view had been monopolar. Pope and
Johnson paired contraries, such as reason and feeling, the one and the
many, the universal and the particular, permanence and change, perfection and imperfection, and then decided which member of each pair
was good. They chose reason, the one, the universal, permanence, and
perfection. "The artist is simply the spokesman of the reason", Arthur
Lovejoy observes of neoclassic aesthetics, "and it is exclusively to the
reason in other men that he must appeal; and 'reason' here is... a name
for that which is fundamental and constant in the generic constitution
of man. The aim of the poet is to express... 'cette beauté qui doit plaire
à tout le monde,' for 'la raison n'est pas sujette au changement'; 'il est
certain,' as Balzac and all the neoclassic writers, in one or another form
of words had declared, 'que la raison est de tout pays'"[14] The Romantic
revolution, however, did not go to the other extreme. The Romantic
writers did not choose feeling, the many, the particular, change, and
imperfection as the good members of each pair. That common view,
rather entrenched still, is too simplistic. The Romantics' view became
dipolar, an 'either *and* or' way of looking at things. They kept *both*
sides separate and together. The key statement is the one we have seen:
The imagination "reveals itself in the balance [duality] or reconciliation
[unity] of opposite or discordant qualities: of sameness, with difference;
of the general, with the concrete; the idea, with the image; the individual,
with the representative", and so on. This new concept of the imagination

[13]  Read, 165.
[14]  *Essays in the History of Ideas* (New York, 1960), 89.

is the poetic corollary of the philosophy or dipolarity: The imagination stands between reason and feeling, between the one and the many, permanence and change, balancing and reconciling them. We have only to remember the passage from Johnson's *Rasselas* (1759) to realize what had happened in less than fifty years: "The business of the poet... is to examine, not the individual, but the species; to remark general properties and large appearances; he does not number the streaks of the tulip, or describe the different shades in the verdure of the forest... He must divest himself of the prejudices of his age or country; he must consider right and wrong in their abstracted and invariable state; he must disregard present laws and opinions, and rise to general and transcendental truths, which will always be the same."[15] Each 'good' member of the pairs is chosen: the species over the individual, the general over the particular, the same over the different. The neoclassic aesthetic consisted of such monopolarizing.

For Johnson there is a definite cleft between the natural and the supernatural: transcendental truths are always the same; particular truths vary and can not be trusted to apply to everyone everywhere. For Coleridge and Wordsworth, though, truth is not a matter of invariability or variability. Its locus is the relationship between the general and the particular; it belongs to neither but resides at once aloof and involved in its two manifestations. In Coleridge's description of the purpose of the *Lyrical Ballads*, this chiastic mode of thought emerges to define what is new in 1798: Wordsworth is to write on natural subjects and supernaturalize them; Coleridge is to write on supernatural subjects and naturalize them. The passage is this:

it was agreed, that my endeavours should be directed to persons and characters supernatural, or at least romantic; yet so as to transfer from our inward nature a human interest and a semblance of truth sufficient to procure for these shadows of imagination that willing suspension of disbelief for the moment, which constitutes poetic faith. Mr. Wordsworth, on the other hand, was to propose to himself as his object, to give the charm of novelty to things of every day, and to excite a feeling analogous to the supernatural, by awakening the mind's attention from the lethargy of custom, and directing it to the loveliness and the wonders of the world... (II, 6)

The Romantic poet does not only set out to naturalize supernaturalism; this notion is another version of the old dichotomy between reason and feeling. He is determined also to supernaturalize the natural. We have

---

[15]   Ed. George Birkbeck Hill (Oxford, 1942), 62-63.

a new idiom, surely, but Wordsworth and Coleridge nevertheless decided through poetic theory and practice to make their work correspond in mutual structure and theme with the idea of truth as dipolar instead of exclusive. And this idea of truth followed from the idea of God as dipolar. God is not simplicity alone, or being alone, but complexity and becoming and change as well. In contrast with Johnson, they say: rise to the general/particular (Coleridge) or the particular/general (Wordsworth) and to transcendental/earthly truths which will always be the same and different. The vehicle is the Romantic imagination which encompasses feeling and thought and is the manifestation in man of the inclusive nature of God. If the stated purpose is to naturalize the super-natural and to supernaturalize the natural, it is so because the mystery of God lies in making his immanence transcendent and his transcendence immanent, making becoming being and being becoming. If Christ had been lost as an image of God (and man), he was found anew for literature in a plethora of literary hypostases through the use of chiasms by all the major Romantic poets. Coleridge and Wordsworth neither emphasize the common nor the uncommon. The truth between is what they aim for and it is to be reflected in the chiastic nature of the *Lyrical Ballads* as a book where the one truth shows its double nature in the opposite but complementary approaches of the two poets. What is new, actually, is the insistence on the reciprocity of the two poets' work, on "the practicability of combining both" (II, 5).

This was in the air of the time and emerged in synchronistic fashion with German philosophy. In Schelling, Coleridge said, "I first found a genial coincidence with much that I had toiled out for myself, and a powerful assistance in what I had yet to do" (I, 102). What he had toiled out was the system of aesthetics we are dealing with, a system which he based on a way of apprehending God: "The primary IMAGINATION I hold to be... a repetition in the finite mind of the eternal act of creation in the infinite I AM" (I, 202). The secondary imagination differs only in degree from the primary imagination; it repeats in art the togetherness and reciprocity of the finite and the infinite.

Schelling's approach to the nature of God is central to the revolution of thought which took place in the Romantic movement. To him, Coleridge wrote, "we owe the completion, and the most important victories, of this revolution in philosophy". "To me", he continues, "it will be happiness and honor enough, should I succeed in rendering the system itself intelligible to my countrymen" (I, 104). The essence of Schelling's approach, refined in a later work *The Ages of the World*, is this: he ceased thinking of God in terms of monopolarity and began thinking of him in terms of dipolarity. God had previously been considered as pure being and pure spirit outside time, necessarily excluding any references of becoming, matter, or time. What Schelling did was bring the second pole of attributes into the nature of God. God was being becoming, timeless in time, material spirit; he was not monopolar but dipolar. The following passages from Schelling's work, *The Ages of the World*, make this clear:

There are thus two principles even in what is necessary in God: the outflowing, outspreading, self-giving essence, and an equally eternal power of selfhood, of return unto self, of being-in-self. Without his further deed, God is in himself both of these, that essence and this power.

It is not enough to see the antithesis; it must also be recognized that these contraries are equally essential and original. The power by which the essence confines itself, denies itself, is in its kind as real as the contrary principle; each has its own root, and neither is to be derived from the other. For if this were to be the case, then the antithesis would again immediately cease. But it is in itself impossible that exact opposites be derived from each other.

The presence of such an eternal antithesis could not escape the first man who felt and perceived intimately. Already finding this duality in the primordial beginnings of nature, but nowhere finding its sources in the visible, he would soon have to say to himself that the basis of the antithesis is as old as, indeed even older than, the world; that, as in all that is living, so already in the primal life there is indeed a doubleness which, descended through many steps, has determined itself as that which appears to us as light and darkness, the male and the female, the spiritual and the corporeal. Therefore precisely the most ancient doctrines represented the first nature as an essence with two modes of action which clash with each other.

Yet it not enough merely to discern the antithesis, if the unity of the essence is not recognized at the same time, or if it is not seen that it is indeed *one and the same* which is the affirmation and the negation, the outspreading and the restraining.[16]

Thus we find that the first nature is of itself in contradiction – not in an accidental contradiction, or one in which it would be placed from without (for there is nothing outside of it), but in a necessary contradiction, posited together with its nature, and which therefore, strictly speaking, is its nature.[17]

In the *Lyrical Ballads* it is also not enough to discern the antithetical approach of Wordsworth and Coleridge. The unity of their endeavor

---

[16]   Trans. and ed. Frederick de Wolfe Bolman, Jr. (New York, 1942), 97-99.
[17]   *Ibid.*, 105.

must also be recognized at the same time. It is the doubleness of the single primal life *(Ursein)* they reveal in their two modes of writing. The dominant theme appears in Coleridge particularly in terms of the male and the female, and in Wordsworth particularly in terms of the spiritual and the corporeal:

> And I have felt
> A presence that disturbs me with the joy
> Of elevated thoughts; a sense sublime
> Of something far more deeply interfused,
> Whose dwelling is the light of setting suns,
> And the round ocean and the living air,
> And the blue sky, and in the mind of man;
> A motion and a spirit, that impels
> All thinking things, all objects of all thought,
> And rolls through all things.

("Tintern Abbey")

The spiritual and the corporeal can not logically be reconciled for the essence of each is the absence of the other. This is logically impossible but not symbol-logically. The idea of logic and contradiction flow from a rationally conceived God. Now, though, God is not conceived but imagined as the "balance or reconciliation of opposite or discordant qualities". His nature is symbolic: it stands between outspreading and restraining just as Coleridge, in imitation, takes his poetic stand between sameness and difference, between the idea and the image.

The following passage, again from *The Ages of the World*, is a succinct statement of just what it is that lies behind the redirection of thought we have chosen to term Romantic:

Everything depends upon comprehending that unity in God which is at the same time duality, or, conversely, the duality which is at the same time unity. If God were identical with his eternal nature or bound to it, then there would only be unity. If both were completely external to each other and separated, then there would only be duality. But the concept of that unity, which, because it is a voluntary one, just on that account encloses a duality, is completely foreign to our era. This era wants only unity and wants to know of nothing but spirit and purest simplicity in God.[18]

---

[18]  Trans. and ed. Bolman, Jr., 157. "Alles kommt darauf an, jene Einheit in Gott zu fassen, die zugleich Zweiheit ist, oder umgekehrt die Zweiheit, welche zugleich Einheit ist. Wäre Gott mit seiner ewigen Natur einerlei oder an sie gebunden, so wäre nur Einheit. Wären beide völlig aussereinander und getrennt, so wäre nur Zweiheit. Aber der Begriff jener Einheit, die, weil sie eine freiwillige ist, eben darum eine Zweiheit einschliesst, ist diesen Zeiten völlig fremd. Diese wollen nur Einheit, und wollen in Gott nichts als Geist und lauterste Einfachheit wissen."

Romanticism is a revolution from that era which "wants only unity and
wants to know of nothing but spirit and purest simplicity in God". Yet
clearly, if it is a revolt against only unity it is also not the revolution of
another era which wants only diversity and wants to know of nothing
but matter and purest variety in God. It is not a revolution from uni-
formitarianism and stasis on behalf of diversitarianism and dynamism.
For Romanticism, everything depends upon comprehending that unity
which is at the same time duality, or conversely, the duality which is at
the same time unity – within works, between works, and within the
*Lyrical Ballads* between the works of two men who dualize unity by
showing the common or human or diverse in what is beyond nature, and
who unify duality by showing the uncommon or supernatural in the
changing many. What Plato said of the wise philosopher can also be said
of the confirmed Romantic poet: he "cannot possibly accept the notion
of those who say that the whole is at rest, either as unity or in many
forms: and he will be utterly deaf to those who assert universal motion.
As children say entreatingly 'Give us both,' so he will include both the
moveable and immoveable in the definition of being and all."[19] Romanticism says: Give us Both. Philosophic and aesthetic, it is monistic dualism
or dualistic monism.

3

Coleridge's attempt to include both the moveable and immoveable in his
definition of being and all gathers ground in the *Biographia Literaria* and
finally culminates in the definition of the imagination. "Now the transcendental philosophy demands", Coleridge wrote in chapter thirteen,
"first, that two forces should be conceived which counteract each other
by their essential nature; not only not in consequence of the accidental
direction of each, but as prior to all direction, nay, as the primary forces
from which the conditions of all possible directions are derivative and
deducible: secondly, that these forces should be assumed to be both
alike infinite, both alike indestructible" (I, 197). Coleridge too thought
the basis of the antithesis was "as old as, indeed older than, the world";
it was the source "from which the conditions of all possible directions
are derivative". Furthermore, like Schelling, he knew that the unity of
the duality, of the antithesis, had to be recognized also. The demands of

19   *The Dialogues of Plato*, trans. and ed. Benjamin Jowett (Oxford, 1964), III, 402.

transcendental philosophy met, "the problem", he states, "will then be to discover the result or product of two such forces, as distinguished from the result of those forces which are finite, and derive their difference solely from the circumstance of their direction". This done, "it will remain for us", he continues, "to elevate the Thesis from notional to actual, by contemplating intuitively this one power with its two inherent indestructible yet counteracting forces, and the results or generations to which their inter-penetration gives existence, in the living principle and in the process of our own self-consciousness" (I, 197-198). The counteraction of the two opposite principles results in a "tertium aliquid" which "can be no other than an inter-penetration of the counteracting powers, partaking of both" (I, 198). Here Coleridge begins to fuse Plato's thoughts with Schelling's but the breath of what is lying in his metaphysical Schwarzwald can begin to be heard. In chapter twelve he calls these forces centrifugal and centripetal; we remember them from Schelling as "the outspreading and the restraining". Specifically identified, they are the motion of the intelligence "in the one... to *objectize* itself, and in the other to *know* itself in the object" (I, 188). Theology has here been transformed into epistemology but the problems of the one are the solutions of the other:

We are to seek therefore for some absolute truth capable of communicating to other positions a certainty, which it has not itself borrowed; a truth self-grounded, unconditional and known by its own light... it must be found in that which is neither subject nor object exclusively, but which is the identity of both.
   This principle... manifests itself in the SUM or I AM; which I shall hereafter indiscriminately express by the words spirit, self, and self-consciousness. In this, and in this alone, object and subject, being and knowing are identical, each involving, and supposing the other. (I, 181-183)

As Arthur Lovejoy has written, "the knower (or the knowing act) and the known, subject and object, must be one; and it seemed obvious that only in self-consciousness can this requirement be satisfied. In this alone we experience being, and find reality by being real."[20] And this is what God does; the principle is, indeed, "a repetition in the finite mind of the eternal act of creation in the infinite I AM". In this way, then, "philosophy would pass into religion", Coleridge said, "and religion become inclusive of philosophy. We begin with I KNOW MYSELF, in order to end with the absolute I AM. We proceed from the SELF, in order to lose and find all self in GOD" (I, 186).

[20]   *The Reason, the Understanding, and Time* (Baltimore, 1961), 48.

We are brought around, finally, to Schelling's ultimate thesis that "the first nature is of itself a contradiction", "is at the same time duality, or, conversely, the duality which is at the same time unity". Thesis VIII is Coleridge's statement of this idea and also an adumbration of the nature of the imagination which is the literary ramification of his theological and philosophic perception:

Whatever in its origin is objective, is likewise as such necessarily finite. Therefore, since the spirit is not originally an object, and as the subject exists in antithesis to an object, the spirit can not originally be finite. But neither can it be a subject without becoming an object, and, *as it is originally the identity of both, it can be conceived neither as infinite nor finite exclusively, but as the most original union of both*. In the existence, *in the reconciling, and the recurrence of this contradiction* consists the process and mystery of production and life. (I, 185, my italics)

Life consists not in reconciliation alone but in the constant recurrence of contradiction as well, in other words in continually renewed balance and difference right in the midst of union and reconciliation. The flash when neither union nor opposition dominates is the moment of mystery at the center of life itself and of the life of the imagination and its products. "Difficult to grasp, and liable to be dismissed as chimerical", wrote Richard Harter Fogle, "the notion of the unifying power could yet be justified, if for no other reason, by its central position in all Coleridge's thinking whether literary, scientific, psychological, metaphysical, or theological".[21] God dipolar, the imagination itself became dipolar. As in God, so in man "there are evidently two powers at work, which relatively to each other are active and passive; and this is not possible without an intermediate faculty, which is at once both active and passive" (I, 86). "In philosophical language", he continues, "we must denominate this intermediate faculty in all its degrees and determinations, the IMAGINATION." The function of this faculty, at once active and passive, is similarly to reconcile: to bring opposites into such unity as – from *The Ages of the World* – "encloses a duality".

Only in this entire context can the full meaning of Coleridge's famous definition of the imagination emerge. He was not talking about an ironic faculty when he said that it reconciles sameness with difference, the general with the concrete, and the idea with the image. It could be seen as such a power easily enough. But we miss half the force and thrill in Coleridge's thought if we concentrate solely on the aesthetics of the

---

[21]   *The Idea of Coleridge's Criticism* (Berkeley, 1962), 19.

imagination. To do this is to go to sleep just when the rockets go off. For Coleridge the imagination echoes the life it was created in the image of, and the works it produces in turn echo it. The work, like its source, the imagination, and like the imagination's source, God, is a "tertium aliquid", a symbolic intersection of the mind interpreting and the matter interpreted. The three – God, the imagination, and the imagined – come together in the trinity that is Coleridge's full conception. The relevant passage is from his essay "On Poesy or Art":

As soon as the human mind is intelligibly addressed by an outward image... so soon does art commence. But please to observe that I have laid particular stress on the words "human mind," – meaning to exclude thereby all results common to man and all other sentient creatures, and consequently confining myself to the effect produced by the congruity of the animal impression with the reflective powers of the mind; so that not the thing presented, but that which is re-presented by the thing, shall be the source of the pleasure. In this sense nature itself is to a religious observer the art of God; and for the same cause art itself might be defined as of a middle quality between a thought and a thing, or, as I said before, the union and reconciliation of that which is nature with that which is exclusively human. (II, 254-255)[22]

The congruity of "the animal impression with the reflective powers of the mind" clarifies what the Romantic meant in his juxtaposition of thought and feeling. Feeling was the concrete thing as it passed impressionally through sensory apparatus in the human body to join midway with the abstract, interpreting mind at the crossroads of the imagination; the resultant was the concrete universal. By the imagination the

---

[22] Cf. Jacques Maritain, *Creative Intuition in Art and Poetry* (New York, 1958), 3: poetry is "that intercommunication between the inner being of things and the inner being of the human Self which is a kind of divination". And this passage on 89-90: "Poetic knowledge is as natural to the spirit of man as the return of the bird to his nest; and it is the universe which, together with the spirit, makes its way back to the mysterious nest of the soul. For the content of poetic intuition is both the reality of the things of the world and the subjectivity of the poet, both obscurely conveyed through an intentional or spiritualized emotion. The soul is known in the experience of the world and the world is known in the experience of the soul, through a knowledge which does not know itself. For such knowledge knows, not in order to know, but in order to produce. It is toward creation that it tends." We are involved here with what Owen Barfield calls "the paradox of inspiration". The passage from his book, *Poetic Diction* (London, 1928), is this: "Such, then, is the paradox of inspiration. The time-honoured 'subjective-objective' dichotomy vanishes in the light of concrete thinking; and the word *concrete* can perhaps best be defined as 'that which is neither objective nor subjective'" (210). From this follows the definition of beauty given by Herbert Langfeld, *The Aesthetic Attitude* (New York, 1920), 108: beauty is "neither subjective nor objective, neither the result of purely intellectual activity, nor a value inherent in the object, but a relation between two variables – the human organism and the object."

dichotomy of Descartes' *res extensa* and *res cogitans* was resolved. It
was resolved symbolistically by being undercut in art. Art is the area in
which the ancient epistemological problem of the separation between
mind and matter was overcome. The concrete was not enough; associated
with change, by itself it was intolerable. Nor was the universal enough;
associated with permanence, by itself it too was intolerable. The metaphysics involved bolstered the conclusion which the philosopher-poet
was determined to have. This coming together of man and his environment (nature), of thought and feeling, of the permanence associated with
man-abstracting in thought and of the change associated with concrete
environment, was a shift in emphasis through implication to man and
nature from God and world. The initial dichotomy was between a
spiritual and permanent God and his material and changing world;
the dichotomy was continued to abstracting-man and his concrete environment. But the postulate that infinite God and finite world (or,
infinite permanence and finite change) were reconciled and balanced in
*Ursein* or Ur-God – "neither as infinite nor finite exclusively, but as the
most original union of both" – was also continued to the balance and
reconciliation of man and nature by the imagination, the Ur-faculty
composed of both. Dichotomy and unity alike were undercut by dual-
union. And the artwork, the imagination expressing itself, also balances
and reconciles such antinomies; it is "a middle quality between a thought
and a thing":

                                        out there
    at the pen's point or brush's tip, do world
    and spirit wed.

    In the confluence of the wrist
    things and ideas ripple together...[23]


4


Coleridge accepted the triangle as "the first and simplest symbol of
multëity in unity" (II, 230). To picture the whole topic we can imagine
a triangle whose apex is God, the left angle Imagination, and the right
angle Poem. What we can call the governing Romantic theorem is this:
the unity of the angle is the sum of the duality of its sides. Thus, God

[23] Howard Nemerov, *New and Selected Poems* (Chicago, 1963), "Writing", 75;
"Painting a Mountain Stream", 57.

conjoins becoming-being; Imagination conjoins world-man; and Poem conjoins particular-universal. Furthermore, each angle contains within itself a subsidiary triangle. Life, at the angle of God, conjoins thesis and antithesis, as God conjoins becoming and being; Taste, at the angle of Imagination, conjoins image and idea, as the imagination conjoins world and man; and Beauty, at the angle of Poem, conjoins the many and the one, as the poem conjoins the particular and the universal. The reconciliation and balance of the real and ideal or change and permanence is the ultimate reason for all other conjunction. The first subsidiary triangle is that of Life: "Life... we consider as the copula, or the unity of thesis and antithesis, position and counterposition, – Life itself being the positive of both; as, on the other hand, the two counterpoints are the necessary conditions of the *manifestations* of Life... Thus, in the identity of the two counterpowers, Life *sub*sists; in their strife it *con*sists: and in their reconciliation it at once dies and is born again into a new form, either falling back into the life of the whole, or starting anew in the process of individuation."[24] God created life and he created life in his own image as "the unity of thesis and antithesis". This was the view of Schelling in whom Coleridge had "found a genial coincidence" with much that he had toiled out for himself. "TASTE is the intermediate faculty which connects the active with the passive powers of our nature, the intellect with the senses; and its appointed function is to elevate the *images* of the latter, while it realizes the *ideas* of the former. We must therefore have learned what is peculiar to each, before we can understand that 'Third something,' which is formed by a harmony of both" (II, 227). It is clear that Coleridge could just as well be writing of God, who is also a "Third something", the permanence of spiritual idea (heaven) and the change of material image (earth). The same principle of dipolarity is at work. The work of art is "a middle quality between a thought and a thing", but once contemplated as such it becomes, in relation to contemplation, thing contemplated by thought. The artwork had united and does unite image with idea; but seen it becomes image in relation to idea. A duality is again re-established out of the very materials the artwork had united. Taste, then, reinforces the imagination and recreates the dual-union (that third something) in aesthetic response. Taste is the imagination functioning as it appreciates the artwork. What it appreciates is the beautiful which "in its essentials, that is, in *kind* and not in *degree*, is that in which the *many*, still seen as many, becomes one... The most

[24]  *The Complete Works*, I, 392.

general definition of beauty, therefore, is... Multëity in Unity" (II, 232).
That is beautiful in which two counterpowers or counterdirections
towards the many and towards the one are conjoined: in which the
particular, still seen as particular, becomes universal. The system is
complete:

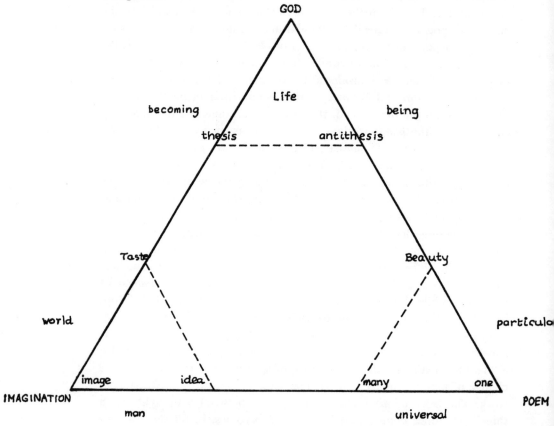

Called idealistic and dismissed as transcendental, Coleridge's thought is
anything but idealism or, better, "only so far idealism", in his own words,
"as it is at the same time, and on that very account, the truest and most
binding realism" (I, 178). The ideal is very definitely one side of the
triangle; but we must not forget that the real is also just as definitely
the other side: the two together are one while remaining two; or the one
is two while remaining one. For Coleridge it is not a matter of logic or
understanding; it is a matter of Reason in the Kantian meaning of that
term, the one Coleridge subscribed to and the essence of which Arthur

Lovejoy has pinpointed in his study of Romantic epistemology, *The Reason, the Understanding, and Time:*

The reasoning characteristic of ordinary thought and natural science depends upon the setting up of sharp contrasts between things, upon propounding dilemmas and formulating irreconcilable oppositions. The Understanding prides itself upon defining issues sharply and then taking sides. Its entire thinking, in short, is based upon the logical principle of contradiction. But the higher insight of the Reason transcends these oppositions. It is all for embracing both sides of all questions. It makes the dialectical lion lie down with the dialectical lamb; it happily enables you, in speculative matters, to eat your cake and have it too. The Reason thus often declares propositions to be true which, so long as you remain upon the lower level of the Understanding, undeniably *seem* flatly self-contradictory.[25]

Coleridge does set up sharp contrasts and oppositions but he does not take sides; or rather he takes both sides, because, as Schelling said, "the first nature is of itself a contradiction". Newton Stallknecht suggests as much when he says that "Coleridge seems to have advocated a type of monistic idealism in some way freed of pantheism. We know from *Biographia Literaria* that, even as late as 1815, he thought such a combination not impossible."[26] The point Nicolas Berdyaev makes is apt here. The relation which subsists among God, the world, and man "certainly should not be taken to mean pantheistic identity. That is always evidence of rationalistic thinking about being in which everything is either relegated to a place outside, or identified with, something. God and man are not external to each other, nor outside one another; neither are they identified, the one nature does not disappear in the other. But it is impossible to work out adequate concepts about this, it can be expressed only in symbols."[27] Coleridge's philosophy is freed from pantheism because God is not identified with real matter; including it, he continues nevertheless as ideal spirit. He is dipolar; the ideal and the real are two lines out from a single angle including both. Coleridge learned this from the German philosophers and from his own speculation. Only with such a philosophy of monistic dualism or dualistic monism – not "monistic idealism" – is "such a combination not impossible".

## 5

Coleridge's statement that "no man was ever yet a great poet, without being at the same time a profound philosopher" (II, 19) is *a fortiori* true

---

[25] Pp. 137-138.
[26] *Strange Seas of Thought* (Bloomington, Ind., 1958), 143.
[27] *The Beginning and the End,* trans. R. M. French (New York, 1957), 101.

of himself. Coleridge undercuts poetically, because he can undercut philosophically, what William Lynch has described as the "long war between the two forms of the imagination", gnostic and Hebraic, "between the men of the finite and the men of the infinite".[28] This long war began in earnest in the fifth century over the nature of Christ. The long verbal wrangles pitted the two-nature men against the one-nature men, and those who emphasized the finite-material with those who emphasized the infinite-spiritual. The Council of Chalcedon resolved the issue in 451. When we read the Council's final decree we realize that the same issues of unity and duality and the spiritual and the material resurfaced in the Romantic era to be resolved by similar language all over again in the philosophy of Schelling and the aesthetics of Coleridge. This explains the peculiarly religious ring of both writers and many others – especially Hegel in philosophy and Wordsworth in literature. The final decree was this:

We declare that the one selfsame Christ, only-begotten Son and Lord, must be acknowledged in two natures [*phýseis*] without any commingling or change or division or separation; that the distinction between the natures [*phýseis*] is in no way removed by their union but rather that the specific character of each nature [*phýsis*] is preserved and they are united in one person [*prósōpon*] and one *hypóstasis*. We declare that he is not split or divided into two persons [*prósōpa*, plural] but that there is one selfsame only-begotten Son, God the Word, the Lord Jesus Christ.[29]

Coleridge tried to be just as exact, we can recall, in Thesis VIII: the spirit, self, or self-consciousness "can be conceived neither as infinite nor finite exclusively, but as the most original union of both". The self, then, is made in the image of Christ, for "we proceed from the SELF, in order to lose and find all self in GOD" (I, 186). The imagination is the self's faculty and reveals the SELF in the incarnate word of poetry. These lines of Nemerov's poem "Carol" are exactly to the point:

> ... there was born at Bethlehem
> *In silence and night*
> The world's and heaven's single stem
> That to both kingdoms we might then
> Say Amen.[30]

In "A Lay Sermon" Coleridge does perceive more than an analogy be-

28   *Christ and Apollo* (New York, 1963), 19.
29   David Bowman, *The Word Made Flesh* (Englewood Cliffs, N. J., 1965), 89.
30   *New and Selected Poems*, 110.

tween the work of the imagination and the word of God. In contrast with
the abstract histories in the nineteenth century, products of the "general
contagion" of "mechanic philosophy", the histories to be found in the
Scriptures are

living educts of the imagination; of that reconciling and mediatory power,
which incorporating the reason in images of the sense, and organizing (as it
were) the flux of the senses by the permanence and self-circling energies of the
reason, gives birth to a system of symbols, harmonious in themselves, and
consubstantial with the truths of which they are the conductors. These are the
*wheels* which Ezekiel beheld... The truths and the symbols that represent them
move in conjunction and form the living chariot that bears up (for us) the
throne of the Divine Humanity. Hence, by a derivative, indeed, but not a
divided, influence, and though in a secondary yet in more than a metaphorical
sense, the Sacred Book is worthily entitled *the Word of God*.[31]

The Word of God manifests his two natures and his one person in the
actual style of the Scriptures for that style is symbolic, and a symbol for
Coleridge "is characterized by a translucence of the special in the individual, or of the general in the special, or of the universal in the general;
above all by the translucence of the eternal through and in the temporal.
It always partakes of the reality which it renders intelligible; and while
it enunciates the whole, abides itself as a living part in that unity of which
it is the representative."[32]

Coleridge's own style in the passage on the Scriptures also partakes of
the reality it renders intelligible. As so many other passages in Romantic
literature (including those more explicit in Lawrence), it contains a submerged sexual analogy to give flesh to the word, to concretize the theme
of difference without division in Scripture and in Christ through the
image of man and woman (two natures, idea and image) in the child born
of their love (one person, the symbol). Thus through the imagination the
permanence of reason is incorporated into images of changing sense to
give birth to the symbol which is *consubstantial* – a Eucharistic word –
with both: the symbol is changing and permanent, an idea and an image,
as a child reflects both parents. The passage, then, by a derivative, but not
a divided, influence, and though in a secondary yet in more than a metaphorical sense, lets us see what it says, for the relationship between
saying and seeing, in the Word-made-Flesh, is the content.[33] Coleridge's

---

[31]  *The Complete Works*, I, 436-437.
[32]  *The Complete Works*, I, 437-438.
[33]  Cf. the Athanasian creed: "Nam sicut anima rationalis et caro unus est homo, ita
deus et homo unus est Christus" (Just as a rational soul and bodily flesh are united in
man, so too god and man are united in Christ).

art here does indeed perform the task he gives it, a task which Hegel echoes in his own similarly charged language:

to represent a spiritual idea to direct contemplation in sensuous form, and not in the form of thought or of pure spirituality. The value and dignity of such representation lies in the correspondence and unity of the two sides, of the spiritual content and its sensuous embodiment, so that the perfection and excellency of art must depend upon the grade of inner harmony and union with which the spiritual idea and the sensuous form interpenetrate.[34]

The interpenetration of the spiritual idea and the sensuous form occurs in symbolic art which is the ineluctable outcome of the philosophy of di-polarity as it expresses itself aesthetically. So Babbalanja, Romantic philosopher of Melville's *Mardi*, describes Lombardo's *Koztanza* as a symbolic work where "matter and mind, though matching not, are mates; and sundered oft... they unite: – the airy waist, embraced by stalwart arms". But this has been prompted by his deeper vision of "things infinite in the finite; and dualities in unities".[35] This idea of art, therefore, as Albert Gérard has written, "has nothing to do with the vague power of suggestion... For the English romantics, the symbol is something more definite: it is a synthesis, a fusion of polarities... In the symbol, the vehicle, which is concrete and singular, and the meaning, which is universal and general, are indissociable and equally essential: they determine each other; their unity is total and indivisible."[36] The concrete and the universal are equally essential because man hungers for the change signified by the one and the permanence signified by the other. To satisfy that yearning – to get the best of THIS WORLD and THAT WORLD, the sensuous and the spiritual – Coleridge joined Schelling and Hegel to assert the world's and heaven's single stem. All at once they said, in the words of Hegel, "the essence of God is the reconciled unity of universality and particularity..."[37] From this all else followed. The same process of dual-oneing was applied to the faculties of man, to man's relationship with the outside world of nature – and to the nature of the imagination and to the nature of poetry.

---

[34]  "The Philosophy of Art", *Hegel: Selections*, ed. Jacob Loewenberg (New York, 1957), 318-319.
[35]  New York, 1963, IV, 328.
[36]  "On the Logic of Romanticism", *Essays in Criticism*, VII (1957), 268.
[37]  *Hegel: Selections*, 317.

# II

# THE POETICS OF ROMANTICISM

## 1. THE CONTRITE CONSCIOUSNESS OF THE ANCIENT MARINER

> There must be a way whereby the word becomes flesh.
> There must be a way whereby the flesh becomes word.
>
> Robert Penn Warren

The myth of the ancient mariner prepares us for the high concentration of "Kubla Khan". It is a dramatic presentation of the human anguish involved in attaining what Kubla so easily decrees. As a myth, the spiritual idea and the sensuous form interpenetrate – Coleridge called it a poem of pure imagination – and the drama of the myth is just that movement in the mariner himself toward what the form of his ballad shows he has attained: a unity of the two aspects of the sensuous and the spiritual. The medium of myth is also clearly his message. He could have given the wedding-guest he stops simply a brief resumé of his experience, but the wedding-guest would have gone directly back to the feast unaffected. He is held, however, by something to which his human nature responds as an echo of its own deep wedding of the sensuous and the spiritual. The mariner appeals neither to the mind of the wedding-guest nor to his emotions. It is his imagination, the focus point of the two counteracting forces of human nature, that is quickened. The ballad makes the wedding-guest see what it says, and in the future he too will feel his thought. The ballad, then, in a secondary yet in more than a metaphorical sense, like the Word of God discussed in "A Lay Sermon", is worthily entitled *The Rime of the Ancient Mariner*. His word manifests what it is about, and the coincidence of moral and manifestation is imaginary truth, and this truth is entirely efficacious. The form of the mariner's telling then, is the direct result of the experience told – the winning of the imaginary view, a victory he is concerned that others attain, although in a secondary way, through the proximity of his poetry to the fact of his life. We have only to listen to realize that "He prayeth best, who loveth best", that there is a single stem between God and man, that they are distinct but inseparable.

In contrast with the old mariner, the young lady Christabel could not see the link between love and prayer; in her case, between sex and religion. That connection was on Coleridge's mind again, for he refers to lines from Crashaw's poem on Saint Theresa which "by some subtle process of the mind" might have suggested "the first thought of the whole poem".[1] As in the Conversation Poems, Coleridge seems to be struggling to bring his own wide love of the world's specifics into the framework of a seemingly orthodox Christianity in which the secular is not the sacred. As for Hawthorne, the prospect is importunate but unsettling, for the idea of God aloof from beanfields and apple-trees is just as strong as the need for rapprochement dictated by the human attachment to things. This is the nature of the mariner's struggle, so close to Coleridge's own in "The Eolian Harp" and "Frost at Midnight", a struggle which does lead to a rapprochement that is confirmed and affirmed in the God-like paradise of Xanadu. But for Christabel there is no resolution: her ascetic up-bringing (1. 332f.) and her impending marriage collide and clash in her mind as we see her hidden self exposed but disguised in Geraldine, the innocent, saintly maiden in a bridal "silken robe of white" about to be sacrificed and ravished by "the tallest of the five" – the dream version of Christabel's "own betrothéd knight", "her lover that's far away". Geraldine's story exposes Christabel's hidden fear of marriage and her refusal to recognize first of all the deep wedding in her own human nature:

> Five warriors seized me yestermorn,
> Me, even me, a maid forlorn:
> They choked my cries with force and fright,
> And tied me on a palfrey white.
>
> . . . . . . . . . . . . . . . . . .
>
> As sure as Heaven shall rescue me,
> I have no thought what men they be;
> Nor do I know how long it is
> (For I have lain entranced I wis)
> Since one, the tallest of the five,
> Took me from the palfrey's back,
> A weary woman, scarce alive.
> Some muttered words his comrades spoke:
> He placed me underneath this oak;
> He swore they would return with haste...              (*Christabel*, ll. 81-98)

---

[1]  *Letters, Conversations, and Recollections* (New York, 1836), 118.

The young good girl Christabel – like her American cousin who also went into the woods late at night (being "But three months married"), Hawthorne's young good man Brown – refuses the proffered lesson that human love and divine love need not be contradictory. Her lover is no more a pimp than Brown's wife Faith is a prostitute, but neither will see this because they have set up sharp contrasts and oppositions according to their familial and social upbringing. Any help, in their view, is the help of the devil. The imagination's revenge is thorough: both Christabel and Young Goodman Brown become the opposites they can not con-join – devils of virtue. By contrast, the mariner does come to imagine but only after he too has set up such contrasts and oppositions between the spiritual and the material. His journey begins with the problem of Christabel and ends with the paradise of Kubla Khan; the mariner spans the two by moving from the one to the other.

The mariner's journey is the way of what Hegel called the Contrite Consciousness. This little section from *Phenomenology of the Spirit* is a philosophic formulation of what Coleridge dramatized in *The Rime of the Ancient Mariner*. As Josiah Royce writes of the essay, the unhappy consciousness "is a phase or stage of consciousness... which is abstract and dualistic in its view of its relation to truth. It is therefore concerned not with external nature, but with its own private ideals, and with a search for personal perfection... together with the goal of this search, namely [the lonely devotee's] far-off 'changeless' or divine consciousness."[2] In the unhappy man there is a conflict between what he considers his True Self, which he identifies with the simple and the changeless, and what he considers his False Self, which he identifies with "the multiform and fickle".[3] The unhappy man is "the unwon unity of the two selves".[4] "The Contrite Consciousness finds these two as mutually estranged. For its own part, because it is the awareness of this contradiction, it takes sides with the Changeless Consciousness, and calls itself the False Self."[5]

This is precisely what happens when the ancient mariner shoots the albatross. This fickle action stirs a belief in him that he is a lost creature remote from the changeless and ideal. At first there is a sense of release and freedom, for the ship moves when the breeze comes up and clears the fog and mist:

[2]  *Hegel: Selections*, 80.
[3]  *Hegel: Selections*, 81.
[4]  *Ibid.*
[5]  *Hegel: Selections*, 81-82.

> Nor dim nor red, like God's own head,
> The glorious Sun uprist:
> Then all averred, I had killed the bird
> That brought the fog and mist.
> 'Twas right, said they, such birds to slay,
> That bring the fog and mist.     (ll. 97-102)

Suddenly, however, a realization of the crime sets in:

> Down dropt the breeze, the sails dropt down,
> 'Twas sad as sad could be;
> And we did speak only to break
> The silence of the sea!     (ll. 107-110)

The sun that was neither dim nor red in rising, and likened to God, is now "bloody" with the mariner's act, at full noon, and motionless:

> All in a hot and copper sky,
> The bloody Sun, at noon,
> Right up above the mast did stand,
> No bigger than the Moon.     (ll. 111-114)

Now the mariner, like the child in "the light of common day" in Wordsworth's "Ode: Intimations of Immortality", is at the equator of his guilt and alone under a God whom he sees mercilessly immoveable. Burdened with guilt and sick for forgiveness from the changeless, the mariner turns from creation as the mirror of his multiform self:

> The very deep did rot: O Christ!
> That ever this should be!
> Yea, slimy things did crawl with legs
> Upon the slimy sea.     (ll. 123-126)

These slimy things are his own fickle impulses which he now abhors. But in turning from what he considers his false self, he also begins to turn from creation. That turning seals the crime because it exacerbates the notion that God dwells as the changeless entirely apart from what he has created – a belief that causes the mariner's own differentiation of his total self into the true self and the false self. There is a hint where he must go before his journey can end in the casual but telling comparison – as an impulsive metaphor – of the sun standing "No bigger than the Moon". The frequency of references to the sun and the moon – twenty-five in all, eleven to the sun and fourteen to the moon – suggests that these bodies externalize the mariner's self-division. References to the moon increase as the mariner begins to heed the voice of what has been to him only the false self. Finally in Part VII there are no references to either, "for the outcome of this process", as Hegel writes, "is precisely the unity of this twofold consciousness".[6]

The mariner begins the journey home to the unity of the twofold consciousness when he accepts his changing self by blessing the snakes he had condemned. Creation's goodness, the realm of change, is now affirmed. The mariner gapes in rapt astonishment and caresses the details of the glittering world he had previously shunned as remote from the changeless:

> Beyond the shadow of the ship,
> I watched the water-snakes:
> They moved in tracks of shining white,
> And when they reared, the elfish light
> Fell off in hoary flakes.
>
> Within the shadow of the ship
> I watched their rich attire:
> Blue, glossy green, and velvet black,
> They coiled and swam; and every track
> Was a flash of golden fire.
>
> O happy living things! no tongue
> Their beauty might declare:
> A spring of love gushed from my heart,
> And I blessed them unaware:
> Sure my kind saint took pity on me,
> And I blessed them unaware.     (ll. 272-287)

Such benediction and acceptance reveal the proximity of the remote, for as the mariner leans towards things in love the albatross falls from his neck and he can pray. The blessing of the snakes is preceded by a preparatory action in the mariner which is figured in the moon:

> The moving Moon went up the sky
> And no where did abide:
> Softly she was going up,
> And a star or two beside –     (ll. 263-266)[7]

The complement of the masculine and remote and stern God in the sun is this feminine and involved and tender God in the moon who sanctions the multiform and the individual, i.e. the false self:

[6] *Hegel: Selections*, 83.
[7] See Mircea Eliade, *Patterns in Comparative Religion*, trans. Rosemary Sheed (Cleveland, 1963) for a discussion of the "Moon-Snake-Rain" pattern in Chapter IV "The Moon and Its Mystique".

Oh sleep! it is a gentle thing,
Beloved from pole to pole!
To Mary Queen the praise be given!
She sent the gentle sleep from Heaven,
That slid into my soul.      (ll. 292-296)

Coleridge's marginal gloss on the moving moon explicitly shows what the
terms of the mariner's conflict have been: "In his loneliness and fixedness
he yearneth towards the journeying Moon, and the stars that still sojourn,
yet still move onward..." All along the conflict has been that of a dissociated sensibility in which fixity, God, the true self, and unity were opposed
to change, the world, the false self, and duality. With the second terms
previously rejected but now at last peacefully embraced, what remains is
to go beyond the sun and the moon into the one that is two as "the stars
that still sojourn, yet still move onward".

The first two stages of the journey of the Contrite Consciousness have
been completed by the mariner: "In the first stage the Changeless appears
to consciousness only as the remote Self [the fixed Sun], that condemns
individuality. In passing through the second stage, consciousness learns
that the Changeless is as much an incarnate individual [the journeying
Moon] as it is itself..." The final stage begins in Part VI in the harbor
and is fulfilled in Part VII when the hermit, who is the whole self, and
also the visible link between God and man, is asked for forgiveness. In
this third stage, in Hegel's words, "consciousness reaches the grade of
the Spirit, rejoices to find itself in the Spirit, and becomes aware that its
individuality is reconciled with the Universal".[8] As Coleridge wrote,
"We proceed from the SELF, in order to lose and find all self in GOD"
(*Biog. Lit.*, I, 186).

The rock and the kirk on the rock, which the mariner sees from the
harbor, image the idea of God as the Changeless. But now, as a result
of the journey, the kirk of God is seen in the softening light of the moon:

The harbour-bay was clear as glass,
So smoothly it was strewn!
And on the bay the moonlight lay,
And the shadow of the Moon.

---

[8]   *Hegel: Selections*, 83. "Das erste Unwandelbare ist ihm nur das fremde, die Einzelheit verurteilende Wesen; indem das andere eine Gestalt der Einzelheit wie es selbst
ist, so wird es drittens zum Geiste, hat sich selbst darin zu finden die Freude und wird
sich, seine Einzelheit mit dem Allgemeinen versöhnt zu sein, bewusst."

The rock shone bright, the kirk no less,
That stands above the rock:
The moonlight steeped in silentness
The steady weathercock.     (ll. 472-479)

In Part VII the hermit appears as the won unity of the two sides which have been at war in the mariner. He objectifies what the mariner has found. As a priest, he represents God and he "kneels at morn, and noon, and eve". But he does so, not apart from life, but totally within life – within the woods and in terms of the rhythm of life and death itself; his prie-dieu is a "cushion plump",

It is the moss that wholly hides
The rotted old oak-stump.     (ll. 521-522)

Here no mention of the moon or of the sun is given. They are not necessary for, as Mircea Eliade has written, "man's integration into the cosmos can only take place if he can bring himself into harmony with the two astral rhythms, 'unifying' the sun and moon in his living body".[9] The mariner still has penance to do but that penance consists in showing to others how he unifies the sun and the moon in himself so that they may do the same. And he does this through poetry – "I have strange power of speech" (l. 587). He has indeed become a priest of the two astral rhythms, and his mythic speech is itself his story. For as art is the "mediator between reason and sensuousness", so too "the Contrite Consciousness stands between the two extremes, at the place where pure thought and the individual consciousness meet. It is in fact itself this meeting place; it is the unity of pure thought and individuality."[10]


## 2. THE TAO OF KUBLA KHAN

one's not half two. It's two are halves of one.

E. E. Cummings


In the introduction to "Kubla Khan", Coleridge describes the three

---

[9]   Eliade, 179. See 184-185: "... in certain Tantric techniques, an attempt is made to 'unify' the moon and the sun, to get beyond the opposition between things, to be reintegrated in the primeval unity. This myth of reintegration is to be found almost everywhere in the history of religion in an infinity of variations – and fundamentally it is an expression of the thirst to abolish dualisms, endless returnings and fragmentary existences."
[10]   *Hegel: Selections*, 87.

hours of profound sleep "in which all the images rose up as *things*, with a parallel production of the correspondent expressions, without any sensation or consciousness of effort".[11] In the dream the image was a thing and that thing gave the exact word to make itself said in such a way that it would also be seen. In the preconscious mind there is no discrepancy between the outer world of fact and the inner world of the psyche: images rise up as things. Poetry is parallel to this dream process for the end of art is "to make the external internal, the internal external, to make nature thought, and thought nature" (*Biog. Lit.*, II, 258). As Anna Balakian observed of Freud, Coleridge too "pointed the way to that substratum of consciousness wherein the distinction between the sensory and the intellectual functioning of the mind is erased", and where "the disparity between the sensory evidence of the outer world and the psychic reality experienced by the mind yields in favor of their inherent unity".[12] The imagination is the faculty of the preconscious and it functions like dream: it incorporates "the reason in images of sense" and "gives birth to a system of symbols" which is the work of art, "the mediatress between, and reconciler of, nature and man" (II, 253). In "Dejection: An Ode", the middle faculty of the imagination is allied to "this strong music in the soul", the "beauty-making power" of joy

> Which wedding Nature to us gives in dower
> A new Earth and new Heaven,
> Undreamt of by the sensual and the proud...       (ll. 68-70)

God and the world no longer form hostile poles just as man no longer stands distant from nature in thought but rather undivided from her, if still distinct, in imagination.

Xanadu is the land of the imagination and its symbolic nature, like that of dream, bridges the gap between thoughts and things. Kubla incorporates his reason in the images of Xanadu, and this incorporation gives birth to a system of symbols which, in descending steps as Schelling said, manifests the doubleness of Kubla's primal life "which appears to us as light and darkness, the male and the female, the spiritual and the corporeal".[13] From the ending of the poem it is clear that Xanadu is more than an exceptional holiday-inn. It is Eden, which literally means *pleasure*, as "pleasure-dome". Coleridge's lines certainly recall Milton's description of Paradise in Book IV of *Paradise Lost:*

---

[11]  *Complete Poetical Works*, ed. Ernest Hartley Coleridge (Oxford, 1957), I, 296.
[12]  *Surrealism: The Road to the Absolute* (New York, 1959), 102.
[13]  *The Ages of the World*, 98.

In this pleasant soil
His far more pleasant garden God ordained.
Out of the fertile ground he caused to grow
All trees of noblest kind for sight, smell, taste...

Southward through Eden went a river large,
Nor changed his course, but through the shaggy hill
Passed underneath ingulfed; for God had thrown
That mountain, as his garden-mould, high raised
Upon the rapid current, which, through veins
Of porous earth with kindly thirst up-drawn,
Rose a fresh fountain, and with many a rill
Watered the garden; thence united fell
Down the steep glade, and met the nether flood...      (ll. 214-231)

And "Kubla Khan" begins:

In Xanadu did Kubla Khan
A stately pleasure-dome decree:
Where Alph, the sacred river, ran
Through caverns measureless to man
Down to a sunless sea.
So twice five miles of fertile ground
With walls and towers were girdled round:
And there were gardens bright with sinuous rills,
Where blossomed many an incense-bearing tree;
And here were forests ancient as the hills,
Enfolding sunny spots of greenery.

The sacred river Alph is also up-drawn as a "mighty fountain" to become
many a rill until it too down the steep grade sinks "in tumult to a lifeless
ocean". Coleridge's poem is a fugue to paradise, the fullness of being,
to the manifestation of the dual and opposite aspects of God's primal
life which man and woman were created in the image of: to the symmetric
restraint of the walls and towers, which circle the fertile ground, but also
to the easy lyricism of the "meandering" river; to the ancient forests
which still enfold young shoots, "sunny spots of greenery"; to the
panting earth and the bursting Alph which begin life on one side, but
also to the caverns of the earth and "sunless sea" which receive it in death
on the other; to the serenity of the "gardens bright with sinuous rills"
as well as to the "ceaseless turmoil" of the "deep romantic chasm".
Life and death, light and dark, height and depth, energy and inertia:
all culminate in the "miracle of rare device", "A sunny pleasure-dome with
caves of ice!" – Mount Abora, the center of the circle and its summary.
    The dome is a mountain, as in Milton's depiction, and not a rural
summer home or Oriental kiosk. The terrain with its ancient forests,

glacial ice caves, and chasms is distinctly mountainous. Furthermore, the Abyssinian maid of Coleridge's vision sings of Mount Abora, and Coleridge says, if he could, that he "would build that dome in air". That dome is clearly, then, Mount Abora. Like Mont Blanc of Shelley's poem, Mount Abora is the source for all other mingled measures. What happens in the center of the temenos, where the mountain stands, happens to everything else within its precinct. The mingled measure of its nature is taken up and played with variations by everything throughout the area. All of creation echoes its source in the mountain whose dome and caves visualize the convex-concave nature of God as "the outflowing, out-spreading, self-giving essence" and as the "equally eternal power of self-hood, of return unto self, of being-in-self".[14] Here at the core of the fugue, the measure is so deeply mingled that thought yields to nature and nature becomes firm with thought in their cross-hatched attributes of sun and ice. What is summarily frozen is as quickly released, and vice-versa; the fugue of order and freedom is perfect. Together, as the he and she of it, the dome and caves of the mountain assert being-becoming and becoming-being.

The movement of the verse itself throughout the poem also echoes the fugue, the mystic measure of God's nature as philosophized by Schelling and here poetized by Coleridge. As Elisabeth Schneider has written, there is a

musical effect in which a smooth, rather swift forward movement is emphasized by the relation of grammatical structure to line and rhyme, yet is impeded and thrown back upon itself even from the beginning by the æ-inclosed line units... In the middle of the poem the slightly stronger forward movement loses itself altogether in the floating equivocation between backward-turned trochaic and forward-leaning iambic movement... In this forward-flowing movement counterpointed against a stationary-oscillating one, form and meaning are almost indistinguishable... The whole poem oscillates between giving and taking away, bright affirmation and sunless negation, light flowing music that nevertheless stands still...[15]

There is no equivocation or ambiguity about this, however. As in the literary tradition of debate between the soul and the body, the backward

---

[14] *The Ages of the World*, 97.
[15] *Coleridge, Opium and "Kubla Khan"* (Chicago, 1953), 286-287. The "*primum datum* in Coleridge's thought", according to Leone Vivante, is just such "creative indeter-minacy": "a *pervading identity*, which is neither a sheer negative nor a sheer positive thing (as objects are bound to be according to the logic of mere existents, or formal logic, which he, as a forerunner, rejected)" (*English Poetry* [Carbondale, Ill., 1963], 124-125).

and forward movements graph the single truth of what both say. Robert
Frost's poem "West-Running Brook" has a similar dialogue of voices
and rhythms to delineate the stream of existence which

> has this throwing backward on itself
> So that the fall of most of it is always
> Raising a little, sending up a little.

Man and woman speak oppositely of the brook in their own singling
away into male and female from the togetherness of backward thought
and forward instinct in the full being of the brook. The brook, as existence
and the law of being and life, includes both their views, in synthesis, as
the conclusion of the playful debate makes clear:

> "It is from this in nature we are from.
> It is most us."
> > "Today will be the day
> You said so."
> > "No, today will be the day
> You said the brook was called West-running Brook."
>
> "Today will be the day of what we both said."[16]

If the backward and forward movements are true to being, they are true
as well to the return unto self and the outflowing from self in Schelling's
conception of God. Coleridge made such movements a principle of
composition, as we would expect from his definition of the imagination:

The reader should be carried forward, not merely or chiefly by the mechanical
impulse of curiosity, or by a restless desire to arrive at the final solution; but
by the pleasureable activity of mind excited by the attractions of the journey
itself. Like the motion of a serpent, which the Egyptians made the emblem
of intellectual power; or like the path of sound through the air; at every step
he pauses and half recedes, and from the retrogressive movement collects the
force which again carries him onward. "Praecipitandus est *liber* spiritus," says
Petronius Arbiter most happily. The epithet, *liber*, here balances the preceding
verb; and it is not easy to conceive more meaning condensed in fewer words.
(*Biog. Lit.*, II, 11)

It is also not easy to conceive more meaning, with movement participating
in the meaning, condensed in fewer words than Coleridge's lines:

> The shadow of the dome of pleasure
> Floated midway on the waves;
> Where was heard the mingled measure

---

[16] *Complete Poems* (New York, 1949) 329.

> From the fountain and the caves.
> It was a miracle of rare device,
> A sunny pleasure dome with caves of ice!

This seemingly contradictory movement is baffling to us in the Western world, but it would be readily understood and appreciated by persons in the East brought up on the *I Ching*. Certainly much of the poem's exotic nature derives from its Eastern quality. The site, after all, is Xanadu. In fact Coleridge captures in the content and in the double movement of his verse the two fundamental principles or forces of yang and yin which are central in Chinese philosophy. These are the undivided line and the divided line which together make Tao, the full measure of heaven and earth: "Yang in movement advances forward; yin in movement draws back."[17] These two concepts form the basis of the Chinese Book of Changes, the *I Ching*, whose "beginnings go back to times when a rational separation of objective from subjective nature did not yet exist".[18] In the *I Ching*, in Coleridge's terms, thought is nature and nature thought. The artist imitates Tao, gets the measure of heaven and earth, by making the internal external and the external internal, in the way "the firm lines [yang] are transformed and become yielding [yin] and the yielding lines [yin] alter and become firm [yang]".[19] Yang and yin, as firm and yielding, are the play in God of aloofness and creativity – the original play which cascades into creation on all levels as the fundamental law of alternating and interacting opposites in nature. They correspond to various and related contraries: yang is the masculine principle whose character originally was a pennant flying in the sun – something bright, later the bright side of the mountain; yin is the feminine principle whose character originally was a cloud – something overshadowing and dark, later the dark side of the mountain. In the play and continual transformation of light and dark (as man and woman, as heaven and earth) the whole truth of Tao emerges:

> It was a miracle of rare device,
> A sunny pleasure dome with caves of ice!

In the middle of Coleridge's poem and at the center of Xanadu, we find the polar forces at the maximum point before transformation. The firm line is being thawed; the yielding line is being frozen. Besides being heard in the rhythm, the two lines are also visualized in the poem in the other

---

[17]  Hellmut Wilhelm, *Change*, trans. Cary F. Baynes (New York, 1964), 83.
[18]  *Change*, 12.
[19]  *Change*, 33.

ways we have seen – the walls and towers, the meandering river; the old forests, the young shoots; the bursting Alph, the sunless sea; the bright and sinuous rills, the savage chasm "athwart a cedarn cover". And central to all is the miracle of Mount Abora, poised between the contraries as firm and yielding, actionless in activity. The imagination has revealed itself in the balance (duality) or reconciliation (unity) of these opposite or discordant qualities. It reveals itself, in Coleridge's words, as active and passive, centrifugal and centripetal. Its source is the deep circle of fertile ground in man, made in God's likeness, where spiritual striving and earth-bound passion coincide. Opposed to the paradise of the imagination is the logical and ruined land of discursiveness, east of Eden, where man's needs are mutually exclusive and estranged. The dilemma of rationality – "Ancestral voices prophesying war" – is posed in Donald Justice's poem "Here in Katmandu". Idea and image, the mountain and the valley, have fallen separately away from their gathering in symbol, *Sinnbild*. Man and woman now quarrel:

> We have climbed the mountain,
> There's nothing more to do.
> It is terrible to come down
> To the valley
> Where, amidst many flowers,
> One thinks of snow,
>
> As, formerly, amidst snow,
> Climbing the mountain,
> One thought of flowers,
> Tremulous, ruddy with dew,
> In the valley.[20]

In Xanadu, however, there are flowers on the mountain and snow in the valley. Kubla has the "simultaneity" which Leone Vivante sees in the first principle, "containing time, as it were, cherishing it, yet nullifying it".[21] He nullifies time in "sunless sea" and "lifeless ocean", but he cherishes it in the starkly sexual and creative force of the chasm from which "a mighty fountain momently was forced". He both cherishes and nullifies time in "That sunny dome! those caves of ice!" Kubla Khan is thus transcendent and immanent – stationary and forward-flowing, yang and yin. In Coleridge's exegesis, the specific character of heaven and earth is preserved even while "they are united in one person [própōson] and one

20  *The Summer Anniversaries* (Middletown, Conn., 1960), 16.
21  *English Poetry*, 106.

hypóstasis".[22] He is the God described by Nicolas Berdyaev as "the perfection of his relation; paradoxically speaking... the absolute perfection of that relation".[23] The sunny pleasure dome with caves of ice is not one thing, but a "Third something" (II, 227) where two are halves of one.

The issue at stake in Schelling's thought and in Coleridge's poem is exactly that raised a long time before them by Plato and by Lao-Tze and probably a long time before them by the first man who yearned for the Incarnation. "O heavens", Plato wrote, "can we ever be made to believe that motion and life and soul and mind are not present with perfect being? Can we imagine that being is devoid of life and mind, and exists in solemn unmeaningness an everlasting fixture?" "That would be a dreadful thing to admit", Theaetetus replies to the Stranger who then concludes: "Under being, then, we must include motion, and that which is moved." Schelling and Coleridge reply with Theaetetus, "Certainly".[24] Through the decree of Kubla Khan, "individuality is made manifest in the Changeless, and... the Changeless is made manifest in individuality".[25] Such ennobling interchange composes the sacred circle of Xanadu in whose center self-sufficiency and self-fecundity mingle as the mystic measure between the fountain and the caves. Coleridge the poet would compose a similar measure if he could revive the dream of the Abyssinian maid who played and sang of Mount Abora. He would have his poetry be like God's poetry. If he could plumb the preconscious, where there is no rational separation between the subjective and the objective, where yielding nature is firm thought and firm thought is yielding nature, he would imitate and recreate God and Tao by reconciling, through the imagination which is passive and active, the idea of backward-turned transcendence with the image of forward-leaning immanence:

> A damsel with a dulcimer
> In a vision once I saw:
> It was an Abyssinian maid,
> And on her dulcimer she played,
> Singing of Mount Abora.
> Could I revive within me
> Her symphony and song,
> To such a deep delight 'twould win me,
> That with music loud and long,
> I would build that dome in air,
> That sunny dome! those caves of ice!

[22] Bowman, *The Word Made Flesh*, 89.
[23] *The Beginning and the End*, 102.
[24] *The Dialogues*, III, 401-402.
[25] *Hegel: Selections*, 83.

The people who heard his poem would see its imaged God. The poet would speak the truth in the Greek sense of the word; he would let us "see something", as Heidegger says, "from the very thing which the discourse is about":[26]

And all who heard should see them there...

He would be the priest of God who sacramentally partakes of God and gives God to others by words which he too makes flesh:

And all should cry, Beware! Beware!
His flashing eyes, his floating hair!
Weave a circle round him thrice,
And close your eyes with holy dread
For he on honey-dew hath fed,
And drunk the milk of Paradise.[27]

The people would behave to him the way Socrates would to "any man who is able to see 'a One and Many' in nature": "him I follow, and 'walk in his footsteps as if he were a god.'"[28]

On many levels for Coleridge, then, as for Robert Frost and for Howard Nemerov in our time,

---

[26] *Being and Time*, trans. John Macquarrie and Edward Robinson (New York, 1962), 56.

[27] Cf. Claude Tresmontant, *Essai sur la Pensée Biblique*, quoted by William Lynch in *Christ and Apollo*, 210-211: "In Biblical metaphysic, God created gratuitously. Time is creation in the act of being accomplished; eternity is the point of view of the creator. Their co-existence is that of the creative action of God and His sufficiency. This is the paradox of the gratuity of creation. The creative action of God co-exists with His repose, His Sabbath... In God, this co-existence of His sufficiency and His Action opens a perspective, demands a hypothesis which the New Testament will come to confirm: God created by love. Thus the Biblical dialectic of time from eternity founds a metaphysic of liberty for human action, and a theology where the reason of all finds itself in love."

"God has created beings who are creators... Human action is creative; it co-exists with divine Action. The latter supports the former, engenders it and pushes it to the plenitude of its autonomy, its liberty: 'You are Gods'. There is an immanence of human action in the Action of God... and inversely immanence of divine Action in human action; the Action of God operates all with regard to our action." This view is part of Morse Peckham's reconsideration of Romanticism: "Man therefore redeems the world; and since in the poet the imagination is predominant, the poet is the primary source of value, in traditional language, redemption. The Romantic poet thus takes upon himself the role of Christ; he becomes Christ, and he is himself his own redeemer and the model for the redemption of mankind. Eventually this task of the artist is extended to every human being" ("Toward a Theory of Romanticism: II. Reconsiderations", *Studies in Romanticism*, I [1961], 6).

[28] *The Dialogues*, III, 174.

Running and standing still at once
is the whole truth.[29]

It was also the whole truth for Plato. In the *Timaeus*, as Arthur Lovejoy explained in *The Great Chain of Being*, we face the concept of "Two-Gods-in-One", "of an Immutability which required, and expressed itself in, Change..." Lovejoy's remarks can serve, I believe, as a reminder that Coleridge's poem is more than a system of delightful sound; that it indeed vitalizes and visualizes an idea whose impact and influence is pervasive in the East and in the West:

And thus Plato, tacitly making the crucial assumption that the existence of many entities not eternal, not supersensible, and far from perfect, was inherently desirable, finds in his other-worldly Absolute, in the Idea of the Good itself, the reason why that Absolute cannot exist alone. The concept of Self-Sufficing Perfection, by a bold logical inversion, was – without losing any of its original implications – converted into the concept of a Self-Transcending Fecundity. A timeless and incorporeal One became the logical ground as well as the dynamic source of the existence of a temporal and material and extremely multiple and variegated universe. The proposition that – as it was phrased in the Middle Ages – *omne bonum est diffusivum sui* here makes its appearance as an axiom of metaphysics. With this reversal there was introduced into European philosophy and theology the combination of ideas that for centuries was to give rise to many of the most characteristic conflicts, the logically and emotionally opposing strains, which mark its history – the conception of (at least) Two-Gods-in-One, of a divine completion which was yet *not* complete in itself since it could not be itself without the existence of beings other than itself and inherently incomplete; of an Immutability which required, and expressed itself in, Change; of an Absolute which was nevertheless not truly absolute because it was related, at least by way of implication and causation, to entities whose nature was not *its* nature and whose existence and perpetual passage were antithetic to its immutable subsistence. The dialectic by which Plato arrives at this combination may seem to many modern ears unconvincing and essentially verbal, and its outcome no better than a contradiction; but we shall fail to understand a large and important part of the subsequent history of ideas in the West if we ignore the fact that just this dual dialectic dominated the thought of many generations, and even more potently in medieval and modern than in ancient times.[30]

The composition of the world-soul, which Plato goes on to describe in the dialogue, also seems to resemble the various interrelated levels of Coleridge's thought. For the composition, Plato seems to struggle with words in the way theologians later did at Chalcedon. Coleridge did once

---

29   Nemerov, "Painting a Mountain Stream", *New and Selected Poems*, 57.
30   *The Great Chain of Being* (Cambridge, Mass., 1957), 49-50.

remark that Jesus Christ was a Platonic philosopher. He might also have added that Plato in turn was a Taoist sage. Here is Plato's version of the undivided and divided lines:

(1) Between the indivisible Existence that is ever in the same state and the divisible Existence that becomes in bodies, he compounded a third form of Existence composed of both.

(2) Again, in the case of Sameness and in that of Difference, he also on the same principle made a compound intermediate between that kind of them which is indivisible and the kind that is divisible in bodies.

(3) Then, taking the three, he blended them all into a unity, forcing the nature of Difference, hard as it was to mingle, into union with Sameness, and mixing them together with Existence.[31]

The language is very familiar. Coleridge's work is indeed like a kind of central power-station: throw any single switch and lights go on in Tübingen, Athens, Jerusalem, and Peking. From God and the imagination of man, Coleridge determines accordingly that in art too, as in "Kubla Khan",

*two elements must coexist, and not only coexist, but must be perceived as co-existing.* These two constituent elements are likeness and unlikeness, or sameness and difference, and in all genuine creations of art there must be a union of these disparates. The artist may take his point of view where he pleases, provided that the desired effect be perceptibly produced, – that there be likeness in the difference, difference in the likeness, *and a reconcilement of both in one.* (II, 256, my italics)

The philosophy of Romanticism determines the poetics. Both represent the emergence of Eastern thought in Western culture. It is an uneasy emergence which needs constant restatement by the poet because Western

---

[31] Trans. Francis M. Cornford (New York, 1959), 24. Cf. the following passage which Jung called "a meaningful exposition of the psychological self": "This Man is a single Monad, uncompounded and indivisible, yet compounded and divisible; loving and at peace with all things yet warring with all things and at war with itself in all things; unlike and like itself, as it were a musical harmony containing all things; ... showing forth all things and giving birth to all things. It is its own mother, its own father, the two immortal names." – *The Collected Works of C. G. Jung,* ed. Sir Herbert Read, Michael Fordham, and Gerhard Adler, trans. R. F. C. Hull (New York, 1957-1963), XIV, 44. The content is comparable to Plato's Two-Gods-in-One, a third form of existence, and to Kubla Khan in Xanadu where "alone are all things at once different and the same"; where "alone, as the principle of all things, does distinction exist unaided by division"; where alone "are will and reason, succession of time and unmoving eternity, infinite change and ineffable rest!" (Coleridge, *The Complete Works,* IV, 41-42).

language divorces the idea and the image in the letter, whereas in the Chinese ideogram or character, in imitation of Tao, the idea and the image coexist and are reconciled. Using the letter given him – "If I could say this to you so you saw" – the Romantic poet nevertheless tries with the tactics available to him (chiefly, making the desire itself the theme and circling it with chiasms and symbiotic contraries) to overcome the division between the idea and the image – a division that linguistically followed in Western culture from the distinction of God as Idea and Spirit divorced from image and matter. In his attempt to remarry thoughts and things, ideas and images, the Romantic poet renews the old attachment and makes manifest the instauration in the primal life of the seminal alliance between in-folding and outspreading, heaven and earth, between the two fundamental principles often metaphorized as man and woman, the indivisible that is firm in eternity and the divisible that yields in time.

### 3. IN DEAR DETAIL BY IDEAL LIGHT: JOHN KEATS

> I never felt at Home – Below –
> And in the Handsome Skies
> I shall not feel at Home – I know –
> I don't like Paradise –
>
> Emily Dickinson

What Coleridge found in philosophy came to John Keats through his youth. In place of "succession of time and unmoving eternity" we find "Their lips touch'd not, but had not bid adieu."[32] Keats might not have read Schelling but he did listen to his pulse and it beat with the same double rhythm of Schelling's God. What might appear as rather arcane in German or Chinese philosophy emerges in his verse with a very human basis: Unity in duality and duality in unity translate into "For ever panting, and for ever young".[33] He staked his poetic claim exactly between two times of human love – before and after. What Coleridge meant by time, for Keats is expectation, and eternity is fulfillment. Both are desirable for him precisely because the one is not the other. His constant strategy, therefore, is to distill them until one loses track of their essential contradiction. Drawing from his studies, in *Endymion* he uses a chemical metaphor for this process:

---

[32]  From "Ode to Psyche", *The Poetical Works*, ed. H. W. Garrod (Oxford, 1958), 263.
[33]  From "Ode on a Grecian Urn".

at the tip-top
There hangs by unseen film, an orbed drop
Of light, and that is love: its influence,
Thrown in our eyes, genders a novel sense,
At which we start and fret; till in the end,
Melting into its radiance, we blend,
Mingle, and so become a part of it...　　(I, ll. 805-811)

"It is almost impossible", as Douglas Bush remarked of his poetry, "to draw a line between sensuous and spiritual experience."[34] Certainly this is the case with these lines, and it is just the effect Keats intended: like André Breton, he found in his verse the secret of loving always for the first time. In his poetry he succeeds again and again in creating a spirit-matter continuum. He is master of what we might call the indicative/ subjunctive: what is, forever also might be. The creation of such a Romantic mood is uniquely his and this is what we respond to in his work – "that magnificent losing struggle to save the body with the soul, to have one's cake as well as watch it being eaten".[35]

For Keats this was the battle of Shakespeare's tragedies. He knew Shakespeare well and what he knew best of all is dramatized in *Troilus and Cressida* – the most Keatsian of Shakespeare's works. For this is the tragedy which says that one can love for the first time but that loving always for the first time is another matter: that dwells with the gods above. Time in the play, with food, defines human limitations. The question Troilus asks in Act III:

What will it be
When that the wat'ry palates taste indeed
Love's thrice-repurèd nectar?　　(ii, 19-21)

is decisively answered in Act V:

The bonds of heaven are slipped, dissolved, and loosed,
And with another knot, five-finger-tied,
The fractions of her faith, orts of her love,
The fragments, scraps, the bits, and greasy relics
Of her o'ereaten faith, are given to Diomed.　　(ii, 153-157)

Keats is poised in the one "flush'd moment, hovering" (*Lamia*, Part I, l. 129), the *Übergangsmoment* between "thrice-repurèd nectar" and "greasy relics". "Hence his recurrent images of stillness and consumma-

---

[34]　*Mythology and the Romantic Tradition* (New York, 1963), 85.
[35]　G. M. Matthews, "The Living Keats", *The New York Review of Books*, XI (November 7, 1968), 30.

tion, the eternal instant before the song ends, the apples drop, the bride
is ravished by quietness; its archetype being the physical act of sex."[36]
As a young man he felt keenly what Emily Dickinson poetized in her
succinct way:

> Partaken – it relieves – indeed –
> But proves us
> That Spices fly
> In the Receipt –[37]

His poetry is an effort to subvert this logic which he felt intensely enough
to try to subvert. The ideal and the actual do contend in his mind, as
Allen Tate remarked,[38] but there can be no question of priority: the one
leads to a "Cold Pastoral" and the other to "A burning forehead".
The problem for him was to switch the adjectives and accidents without
changing the substance in order to effect what Georges Poulet has called
an "earthly eternity" with its auxiliary "feeling of living in another
time-world, in which duration is not successive but permanent".[39] Sonnet
X is one example of this desire:

> O that a week could be an age, and we
>     Felt parting and warm meeting every week,
> Then one poor year a thousand years would be,
>     The flush of welcome ever on the cheek:
> So could we live long life in little space,
>     So time itself would be annihilate,
> So a day's journey in oblivious haze
>     To serve our joys would lengthen and dilate.
> O to arrive each Monday morn from Ind!
>     To land each Tuesday from the rich Levant!
> In little time a host of joys to bind,
>     And keep our souls in one eternal pant!
> This morn, my friend, and yester evening taught
> Me how to harbour such a happy thought.

In an expansive mood, Keats called such a happy thought the game of
"nice-cut-core":

[36] *Ibid.*
[37] *Final Harvest*, ed. Thomas H. Johnson (Boston, 1961), 103.
[38] *The Man of Letters in the Modern World* (New York, 1958), 207.
[39] "Timelessness and Romanticism", *Journal of the History of Ideas*, XV (1954), 17, 6.
Cf. David Perkins, *The Quest for Permanence* (Cambridge, Mass., 1959), 215: "Thus
a paradox is involved. The desire is to get outside of time, but ultimately the only
satisfaction of this desire which is at all possible derives from the momentary sense of
timelessness arising during intense experience in time." The desire is not really to get
outside of time but to take time into eternity. Keats would have duration but per-
manently. The quest is for permanence *and* change. See note 54.

Will you play once more at nice-cut-core,
For it only will last our youth out,
And we have the prime of the kissing time,
We have not one sweet tooth out.

There's a sigh for aye, and a sigh for nay,
And a sigh for I can't bear it!
O what can be done, shall we stay or run?
O cut the sweet apple and share it![40]

For him too, apparently, running and standing still at once is the nice-cut-core of the whole truth. This is what he would teach us to harbor. No more than Theaetetus could Keats wholeheartedly endorse either the immoveable or moveable. At this moment it is not a matter of being, though, but of a kiss. That is enough of a truth for him, and it does give flesh to Plato's words. If we lack examples in Plato or in Schelling for the desire behind unity in duality, they are plentiful in Keats:

Happy is England! I could be content
    To see no other verdure than its own;
    To feel no other breezes than are blown
Through its tall woods with high romances blent:
Yet do I sometimes feel a languishment
    For skies Italian, and an inward groan
    To sit upon an Alp as on a throne,
And half forget what world or worlding meant.
Happy is England, sweet her artless daughters;
    Enough their simple loveliness for me,
        Enough their whitest arms in silence clinging:
Yet do I often warmly burn to see
    Beauties of deeper glance, and hear their singing,
And float with them about the summer waters.

The poem visualizes an attitude which everyone has on his own terms at one time or another. But Keats nourished this attitude all the time. William Lynch puts it very well:

We are all driven by a need for maximum beauty and insight, and at the same time we wish for a habitation in the inescapable minima of human life. Yet we cannot tolerate a permanent dissociation between the two. We wish on the one hand to grasp "meaning" to the full, so that there is no pain of questioning left; on the other hand we have an equal longing for pure, unalloyed, concrete objects, and for not having to go beyond them to get at meaning, joy, or illumination. This double longing exists in all of us. We want the unlimited and the dream, and we also want the earth.[41]

[40]  "O blush not so! O blush not so!" *The Poetical Works*, 544.
[41]  *Christ and Apollo*, 29-30.

For Keats drowsiness is the condition in which one may satisfy the
double longing for the fact and for the dream. His poetry has many
syntactic equivalents of such drowsiness where dream is given a touch of
fact and fact is given a touch of dream. The half-way or *Übergangsmoment*
in love applies with equal force to every kind of experience which he
wants to capture exactly between potency and act. The following lines
from various poems are typical:

1  The God on half-shut feathers sank serene
2  the guarded nymph near-smiling on the green
3  She dwelt but half retir'd
4  A little noiseless noise among the leaves
5  Who can forget her half retiring sweets
6  To woo sweet kisses from averted faces
7  Warm breath, light whisper, tender semi-tone
8  Many such eves of gently whisp'ring noise
9  And she her half-discover'd revels keeping
10  Nymph of the downward smile, and sidelong glance
11  Sappho's meek head was there half smiling down
12  And half discovered wings
13  Among the bushes half leafless[42]

The best example of such nice-cut-core is the "Bright Star" sonnet. The
theme reminds us of St. Augustine's remark, "I want to be a virgin but
not right now":

Bright star! would I were steadfast as thou art –
    Not in lone splendour hung aloft the night
And watching, with eternal lids apart,
    Like nature's patient, sleepless Eremite,
The moving waters at their priestlike task
    Of pure ablution round earth's human shores,
Or gazing on the new soft fallen mask
    Of snow upon the mountains and the moors –
No – yet still steadfast, still unchangeable,
    Pillow'd upon my fair love's ripening breast,
To feel for ever its soft fall and swell,
    Awake for ever in a sweet unrest,
Still, still to hear her tender-taken breath,
And so live ever – or else swoon to death.

The poem is a statement of conflicting desires which resolves itself by
structure. The core that must be cut nicely is that of truth and beauty
in one of their manifestations as purity and essence, love and existence.

[42] *The Poetical Works*, 1 and 2: 194; 3: 199; 4: 3; 5: 27; 6: 54; 7: 473; 8: 43; 9: 39;
10: 42; 11: 60; 12: 46; 13: 44.

It is a delicate cut because the substance of the star cannot exist without the accidents of aloofness, eternity, spirituality; and the substance of love cannot exist with them. Still, like the children Plato mentions, Keats says entreatingly, Give me Both. He must somehow make truth beauty and beauty truth. He wins both through the middle of the poem where a structural process of incarnation moves steadfastness down from the star to the act of love. Keats lets his aversion to the accidents of the star organically take him where they will, and they take him to the "moving waters" "round earth's human shores" and to the "snow upon the mountains". Both are still related to the star by way of "priestlike", "ablution", the height of the mountain and the purity of snow, but they are also now irretrievably bound to earth by the same mediating words. Keats can therefore conclude:

> still steadfast, still unchangeable,
> Pillow'd upon my fair love's ripening breast...

The last line of the poem's first version underscored the synthesis: "*Half-passionless, and so swoon on to death*" (my italics). Love, then, is both idealized and realized, chastity kept and lost, consummation fulfilled while it continues expected. The sonnet does what Keats had done in the cathedral at Chichester for the same conflicting desires: "When a letter came from Fanny Brawne shortly after his arrival, he took it to read walking up and down the aisles during the service in the choir, to his great and secret delight."[43] He was in church all right, but the prayer he read was a love letter. The poem too is "love's missal".

The "Bright Star" sonnet may be used as a propaedeutic poem for what Keats did more elaborately in his longer works. In the sonnet, as in the "Solution sweet" of The Eve of St. Agnes, he steers clear of what Kierkegaard called the despair of finitude which informs Lamia in Lycius' loss of the sense of raptness in Being and being-alive. Lamia becomes in time simply another woman, a property, instead of the secret at the heart of things which she is for Lycius in his young love. The purple palace of his youthful vision fades into just another building in the adult and daylight world of Corinth:

> His spirit pass'd beyond its golden bourn
> Into the noisy world almost forsworn     (Part II, ll. 32-33)

And in the sonnet Keats equally steers clear of the opposite despair of infinitude which pervades Endymion. Endymion hovers above himself as

---

[43]  Aileen Ward, *John Keats: The Making of a Poet* (New York, 1967), 243.

the intellectual esthete in search of essence. He therefore sins against Pan who "wanderest at eventide / Through sunny meadows" (I, ll. 249-250). Pan is the God of heaven and earth, as the chiastic ritual of his priest, in imitation of his hypostasis, makes clear:

> Thus ending, on the shrine he heap'd a spire
> Of teeming sweets, enkindling sacred fire;
> Anon he stain'd the thick and spongy sod
> With wine, in honour of the shepherd-god.     (I, ll. 223-226)

Like the bread and wine in the sacrifice of the Mass, the spire of sweets as a sign of earth is offered up to heaven; and wine, the sign of heaven, is given down to earth – the one to honor Man-God and the other to honor God-Man. But Endymion wants to know of nothing but spirit and purest simplicity in God. D. H. Lawrence's words, from the essay "Pan in America", describe Endymion's career until at last, like the ancient mariner he meets (III, ll. 251-262), Endymion too finds the universal when he accepts the particular. First, though, "he discovered the 'idea'":

This was the death of the great Pan. The idea and the engine came between man and all things, like a death. The old connexion, the old Allness, was severed... We need the universe to live again, so that we can live with it. A conquered universe, a dead Pan, leaves us nothing to live with. You have to abandon the conquest, before Pan will live again. You have to live to live, not to conquer. What's the good of conquering even the North Pole, if after the conquest you've nothing left but an inert fact? Better leave it a mystery.[44]

In his quest for infinitude, Endymion severs the old Allness of the infinite-finite, just as Lycius (through Apollonius) severs it for the finite. In either case the world becomes polluted; there is nothing left to live with for mystery has become problem, and being has become having. The two works could easily appear under the rubric: Keats on Ecology. Here are the pertinent lines:

> There was an awful rainbow once in heaven:
> We know her woof, her texture; she is given
> In the dull catalogue of common things.
> Philosophy will clip an Angel's wings,
> Conquer all mysteries by rule and line
> Empty the haunted air, and gnomed mine –
> Unweave a rainbow, as it erewhile made
> The tender-person'd Lamia melt into a shade.
>
> (*Lamia*, Part II, ll. 231-238)

---

[44]   *Phoenix: The Posthumous Papers of D. H. Lawrence*, ed. Edward D. McDonald (New York, 1936), 29.

Away I wander'd – all the pleasant hues
Of heaven and earth had faded: deepest shades
Were deepest dungeons: heaths and sunny glades
Were full of pestilent light; our taintless rills
Seem'd sooty, and o'er-spread with upturn'd gills
of dying fish...                          (*Endymion*, I. ll. 691-696)[45]


The test of nice-cut-core can be applied to Endymion, to Lycius, to
Porphyro, and to the knight in "La Belle Dame sans Merci". It seems to
be the foundation of the major poems, not only in theme but frequently
in language and often in rhyme – as in the odes where Keats combines
the Petrarchan and Shakespearean patterns to avoid the defects of each
without the other and to gain the virtues of both (restraint and expansive-
ness) together. The fuller implications of the test are revealed in Kierkegaard's philosophical formulation. The language is incarnational and
Romantic:

The self is the conscious synthesis of infinitude and finitude which relates itself
to itself, whose task is to become itself, a task which can be performed only by
means of a relationship to God. But to become oneself is to become concrete.
But to become concrete means neither to become finite nor infinite, for that
which is to become concrete is a synthesis. Accordingly, the development
consists in moving away from oneself infinitely by the process of infinitizing
oneself, and in returning to oneself infinitely by the process of finitizing. If on
the contrary, the self does not become itself, it is in despair, whether it knows
it or not.[46]

The process of infinitizing and the process of finitizing occur together
in the synthesis of the "Bright Star" sonnet. The concrete view appears

---

45   Cf. Shelley, *Prometheus Unbound*, Act I, ll. 542-553:

Dost thou boast the clear knowledge thou waken'dst for man?
Then was kindled within him a thirst which outran
Those perishing waters; a thirst of fierce fever,
Hope, love, doubt, desire, which consume him for ever.
    One came forth of gentle worth
    Smiling on the sanguine earth;
    His words outlived him, like swift poison
    Withering up truth, peace, and pity.
    Look! where round the wide horizon
    Many a million-peopled city
    Vomits smoke in the bright air.
    Hark that outcry of despair!

46   *Fear and Trembling, The Sickness unto Death*, trans. Walter Lowrie (Garden City,
N.Y., 1954), 162-163. Cf. Coleridge, Thesis VIII, quoted above on p. 14. For errors
on either side of Kierkegaard's formulation, see William Lynch, *Images of Hope*
(New York, 1966), 47.

fully in the ode "To Autumn" and in "Ode on a Grecian Urn". In the latter, aware of his own dying youth and the dying of Pan in a steadily polluted England, he looks back towards the old connexion, the old Allness of Greece.

In "Ode on a Grecian Urn" he is again at work on nice-cut-core for he found in Greek culture, manifested in the Elgin Marbles, "the religion of joy" that was his own. Aileen Ward's description of his response to the Elgin Marbles defines their importance to him:

He was struck almost at once by the contemporaneousness of the sculpture – the freshness and vitality which made all copies look ancient and lifeless by contrast. Like Haydon, Keats immediately recognized the profound knowledge of anatomy shaping bone and muscle and tendon in these forms. But he was far more deeply moved by the surging energy of the young horsemen, the robust grace of the maidens, the magnificent serenity of the gods and goddesses. This was the Greek spirit made flesh, 'the religion of joy' he once called it, an embodiment of a religious attitude which he now realized more clearly than ever was his own. A few months later, on one of his many trips back to the museum, he told Severn, 'I never cease to wonder at all that incarnate delight.'[47]

Such incarnate delight is the subject of the poem. In the ode Keats seeks to make the Greek spirit flesh. There was one main difficulty and he was very aware of it: he was not sculpting, he was writing. And he does seem concerned with the difference. He calls the urn a "Sylvan historian" and says that it expresses "A flowery tale more sweetly than our rhyme". Why is it sweeter? Keats seems to demand that such questions be asked to involve us in his own wonder. The questions suggest that poetry ("our rhyme") vis-à-vis sculpture is a dominant concern and that one of Keats's purposes is to reveal the culture which makes such a sweeter art. Calling the urn's tale sweeter, Keats realizes that his own ode, unlike the urn's, refers to something other than itself: words are not things. On the other hand, in an earlier culture, Greek culture, art was not about something outside itself; it was what it was about – at least more than his poem can be. The flowers on the urn are sweeter because they look like flowers. There is nothing flowery, however, about the word *flower*. The urn is the consummate historian because the rural life it renders it also participates in as "Sylvan" and "leaf-fring'd". The phrase hints at a contrast with the printed page or the bound book, language itself, which can only tell abstractly of other things no matter how concrete the vocabulary may be.[48]

---

[47]  *John Keats: The Making of a Poet*, 104.
[48]  Cf. Ernst Cassirer, *Language and Myth*, 12: "Language could not begin with any phase of 'noun concepts' or 'verb concepts', but is the very agency that produces the

The first difference, then, involves forms of art – Keats's written ode, the urn's sculpted ode. Since the work considered is Grecian, the poem discovers and reenacts forces in Greek culture (later identified by Nietzsche as Apollonian and Dionysian) which worked in harmony to produce such art where truth is beauty, where, that is, the distance between ideas and things, so widened by the printed word Keats uses, is dissolved. In the first stanza, therefore, Keats purposely portrays the bent of his own mind as different from the Greek mind. He pictures himself almost frantically looking for an answer and searching for a proposition:

> What leaf-fring'd legend haunts about thy shape
> Of deities or mortals, or of both,
> In Tempe or the dales of Arcady?
> What men or gods are these? What maidens loth?
> What mad pursuit? What struggle to escape?
> What pipes and timbrels? What wild ecstasy?

These questions are asked to tell us what some of the scenes on the urn are, but also to establish by the mood of hectic interrogation the difference between Greek culture and our own. Truth for us, as Martin Heidegger has argued in *An Introduction to Metaphysics* and in *Being and Time*, is a matter of the mind, but this was not so, he maintains, for Greek culture before Plato's *Republic:* "It was in the Sophists and in Plato that appearance was declared to be mere appearance and thus degraded. At the same time being, as *idea*, was exalted to a suprasensory realm."[49] In the *Republic* Plato made truth intellectual for Western civilization after him whereas before it was a matter of manifestation: what exists reveals itself and that revelation is truth. Certainly Keats, as his letter of 22 November 1817 shows, was anxiously trying to get behind or before Plato even while using the Platonic vocabulary he inherits. The remarks in the letter to Benjamin Bailey are helpful because they seem to furnish hints for what the poem does in another way: "What the imagination seizes as Beauty must be truth – whether it existed before or not – for I have the same Idea of all our Passions as of Love they are all in their sublime, creative of essential Beauty."[50] While Keats does posit two different realms, he

distinction between these forms, that introduces the great spiritual 'crisis' in which the permanent is opposed to the transient, and Being is made the contrary of Becoming." See Marshall McLuhan, *Understanding Media* (New York, 1965), Chapter 18 "The Printed Word".

[49] *An Introduction to Metaphysics*, trans. Ralph Manheim (Garden City, N.Y., 1961), 89.

[50] *The Letters*, ed. Hyder Rollins (Cambridge, Mass., 1958), I, 184.

does so only to make it clear that he wishes above all to give human
passions and creativity the same status which essential ideas have in
Plato. He uses the geography of Plato to argue for the equality of existence.
Similarly, the poem depicts Greek culture before Plato's division and
shows the harmony between deities and mortals, between human love
and religious rite which the *Republic* drove apart by relegating human
existence to a secondary position: God's in his heaven; all's shadowy
with the world.[51] The force of Keats's interrogation of the urn in the
first stanza establishes at once a sense of a way of life less divisive than
ours, a way of life that both excites and perplexes the poet. He is perplexed because he is used to keeping, with the rest of us, deities and mortals or ideas and things apart. He is excited because there does not seem
to be such a division on the urn. Its nature touches being itself "whose
essence", in Heidegger's account, "is *logos*, the collectedness of the
conflicting".[52]

Emboldened by the fusion of realms on the urn, Keats proceeds in
the second stanza to a hortatory position. He encourages the human
also to become divine:

> Heard melodies are sweet, but those unheard
> Are sweeter; therefore, ye soft pipes, play on;
> Not to the sensual ear, but, more endear'd,
> Pipe to the spirit ditties of no tone...

After this prayerful use of music, the rest of the stanza shows the desired
deed accomplished. The realm of existence (piping, blooming, loving)
now dovetails with the realm of essence:

> Fair youth, beneath the trees, thou canst not leave
> Thy song, nor ever can those trees be bare;
> Bold Lover, never, never canst thou kiss,
> Though winning near the goal – yet, do not grieve;
> She cannot fade, though thou hast not thy bliss,
> For ever wilt thou love, and she be fair!

In the terms of Keats's letter, human passions have now become "in
their sublime, creative of essential Beauty". The third stanza records
through exclamation the ecstatic identification of Keats with the continuum the urn manifests. In one sense Keats makes the urn what it

---

[51]   Writing of the philosophers before Plato, Heidegger says: "But for the Greeks
standing-in-itself was nothing other than standing-there, standing-in-the-light. Being
means appearing. Appearing is not something subsequent that sometimes happens to
being. Appearing is the very essence of being" (*An Introduction to Metaphysics*, 86).
[52]   *An Introduction to Metaphysics*, 148.

appears to be through the urgency of his own desires to unify the essential and the existential; but in another sense the strength of his desires to elevate human passions admits him to the nature of this sculpture from an earlier time when such desire was fact. Indeed, subjectivity and objectivity – a late distinction – also coalesce here:[53]

> Ah, happy, happy boughs! that cannot shed
> Your leaves, nor ever bid the Spring adieu;
> And, happy melodist, unwearied,
> For ever piping songs for ever new;
> More happy love! more happy, happy love!
> For ever warm and still to be enjoy'd,
> For ever panting, and for ever young;
> All breathing human passion far above,
> That leaves a heart high-sorrowful and cloy'd,
> A burning forehead, and a parching tongue.

We are not without earth in this heaven because although the boughs cannot shed their leaves they are nevertheless still boughs. And although the love is "For ever" it is also "warm" and "panting". The love is above "breathing human passion" not because it is without passion – the previous lines make that clear – but because such human passion is now essential. The love that can begin only because of time is kept and asserted, and then time itself is stopped while the love initiated because of it continues without duration. Time and eternity or change and permanence are thus equally desired although antipodal and contradictory to thought after Plato which the urn's history precedes.[54] Truly the poem is a "disclosure of being", "the unlocking of what forgetfulness of being closes and hides";[55] for "the meaning of 'being' remains within

---

[53] Cf. Jacques Maritain, *Creative Intuition in Art and Poetry*, 83: "the primary requirement of poetry, which is the obscure knowing, by the poet, of his own subjectivity, is inseparable from, is one with another requirement – the grasping, by the poet, of the objective reality of the outer and inner world: not by means of concepts and conceptual knowledge, but by means of... knowledge through affective union."

[54] Cf. James Benziger, *Images of Eternity* (Carbondale, Ill., 1964), 116-117: "Religion has suffered severely in the past few centuries from that ceaseless striving of intellect which Keats' faith in imagination sought to counter. Christianity itself has always had, at least in abeyance, its own doctrine of the ultimate 'resurrection of the body,' presumably in some spiritualized form. If there is any future life, any 'immortality,' if man is to preserve any of that individual personality which religion has insisted he does preserve, such a future is hardly to be imagined without some equivalent of his present corporeal existence as we know it... The traditional doctrine of an historic Incarnation offered such a point of meeting between the corporeal and the wholly spiritual as Keats sought. For that very reason orthodoxy may feel some sympathy for Keats's instinctive insistence upon the 'imaginableness' of truth."

[55] Heidegger, *An Introduction to Metaphysics*, 16.

the sphere of actuality and presence, of permanence and duration, of abiding and occurrence".[56] On the urn heaven and earth meet in what Keats called "the space between" (*Endymion*, I, 1. 301) where deities and mortals unite. In this earlier Greek culture which the urn reveals to us, and which we have lost by thinking logically instead of mythically and symbolically, divisions had no validity because they were literally inconceivable.

This brings us to the fourth stanza which, with the final one, seems to imply a more critical attitude towards the urn which Keats has so far celebrated. This is the sestet of the fourth stanza:

> What little town by river or sea shore,
> Or mountain-built with peaceful citadel,
> Is emptied of this folk, this pious morn?
> And, little town, thy streets for evermore
> Will silent be; and not a soul to tell
> Why thou art desolate, can e'er return.

Here there is permanence, just such permanence summoned in the second stanza to assist change from becoming past. But what was assistance then is contradiction now: with permanence there can be no change; no one can ever return to the little town. Keats therefore presumably finds the sculpture deficient in some ways however appealing in others it might be. It seems more likely, however, that Keats is not being critical of the urn but presenting again the logical and divisive attitude of the first stanza. Facing the urn at first, he then experiences its life, and now is on the other side of that experience looking back. Indeed by such contrast the final two stanzas enshrine all the more what the urn fully is in the third stanza. There Platonic laws of division and contradiction simply do not apply. But they are assumed by Keats again to let us see and hear our own sad distance from symbolic time. In the first and last stanzas, Keats knows from without and -of; in the middle he knows from within and -with. There is no reason to suppose that we should side with discursive confrontation against poetic intuition. On the contrary: to believe that Keats is in fact critical of the urn posits the kind of analytical thinking which these lines assume for contrast with the mythical mode. The designation of the final stanzas as ironical boomerangs in Keats's Grecian strategy.

It is Grecian strategy because in the final stanza, quite distant and

---

[56]  Heidegger, 77.

philosophical, a kind of Apollonian calm prevails as opposed to the Dionysian effervescence of the first stanza's sestet:

> O Attic shape! Fair attitude! with brede
> Of marble men and maidens overwrought,
> With forest branches and the trodden weed;
> Thou, silent form, dost tease us out of thought
> As doth eternity: Cold Pastoral!

These two moods, one at the beginning of the poem and the other at the end, meet in the middle of the poem, the *Berührungspunkt*, where we are indeed teased out of logical thought in the lines "For ever piping songs for ever new", "For ever panting, and for ever young". Here Greek civilization, which the urn typifies and summarizes, consists in a balance between Apollonian and Dionysian forces which in thought become separated and even hostile as spirituality and passion.

If Keats first saw sculpture as superior to poetry, he has overcome the difference through the use of time in marking his own experience. The attitude before the urn is experienced in its fullness, recreates one element of that fullness (the Dionysian); the attitude after recreates the other (the Apollonian). In reading the poem in time, therefore, we too are made to realize the difference between our own categorical viewpoint and that of an inclusive Greek culture which we are also enabled to realize as the middle of the poem where the end of the beginning and the beginning of the end touch and spark a synthesis. From the dynamics of the poem, then, the assertion that "Beauty is truth, truth beauty" is not an enigma at all to be labored over endlessly. Truth and beauty come to each other in "for ever young" from the halves of the poem which are concrete and personal manifestations (first engagement and later reflection) of what broke away from the fullness of being through a later logic which art and the aesthetic experience of art antedate – heaven and earth, eternity and time, permanence and change.[57]

The poem is, then, about another art-form, sculpture, and about the way of life which the sculpture embodies. By means of his chosen strategy of movement in time and tone, Keats gives his poem the immediacy of the Greek work and at the same time effectively defines our distance from

---

[57] The urn, beauty, and truth appear in Shakespeare's poem "The Phoenix and the Turtle". The theme is Keats's favorite – "married chastity". Edward Hubler suggests that the poem may be "Shakespeare's allegory of love". It expounds "the mystical concept of unity in duality, two distinct beings who are nonetheless one" (*Shakespeare's Songs and Poems* [New York, 1959], xlvii and xlvix).

such a life where, to quote the contemporary American poet William
Stafford, we find

> an imagined place
> Where finally the way the world feels
> really means how things are,
> in dear detail,
> by ideal light all around us.[58]

---

[58]  *Traveling through the Dark* (New York, 1962), 92.

# PART TWO

# III

# AMERICANIZING ROMANTICISM

## 1. EMERSON ON PLATO

A Greek head on right Yankee shoulders, whose range
Has Olympus for one pole, for t'other the Exchange.

James Russell Lowell

The idealists dismiss Emerson as a pragmatist and the pragmatists dismiss him as an idealist. It is safe to say that one is wrong, but it is safer to say that both are right. Newton Arvin's remark that Emerson is "a polarized, a contradictory, writer"[1] echoes Robert Pollock's statement that he "resists easy classification".[2] Yet he has been classified, and all too readily classified, but what does the reader do when he discovers that two opposite philosophies claim him, and not as a minor spokesman, at that, but indeed as a great forerunner of their respective heresies? He brushes him off as a sincere but befuddled thinker. It only depends on how you choose your quotations, as William James was well aware when he chose his.[3] Emerson is like the long-bearded Druid in Wordsworth's *Prelude* (XIII, 1. 345 f.): he points alternately to the starry sky and to the plain below. The compass of his wand is the circumference of his philosophy – transcendentalism. As F. O. Matthiessen points out (and our attitude has not changed significantly since the *American Renaissance*), "He did not want his idealism to be divorced from the material facts of his age."[4]

---

[1]   "The House of Pain: Emerson and the Tragic Sense", *Hudson Review*, XII (1959), 51.
[2]   "A Reappraisal of Emerson", *Thought*, XXXII (1957), 86.
[3]   "All these passages appealed to James as celebrating 'pragmatism,' or 'the superiority of action.' But he found these mixed with other passages which declared 'the superiority of what is intellectualized.' Therefore he indexed the two contrasting series of statements, and referred specifically to certain paragraphs which contained 'both close together'" (Frederic I. Carpenter, "William James and Emerson", *American Literature*, XI [1939], 43).
[4]   New York, 1941, 11.

Emerson foresaw, as he did so many other things, how the modern student would reply: "And thus, O circular philosopher, I hear some reader exclaim."[5] "Which did Emerson consider superior", asks Frederic Carpenter, "deeds or thoughts; actions or ideas?"[6] And Melville seems to score the same polarity in *The Confidence-Man:* "And moonshiny as it in theory may be, yet a very practical philosophy it turns out in effect..."[7] This view, as many critics confess, has conditioned our response against Emerson. There is the attack from Yvor Winters in *Maule's Curse*: "Emerson's guiding spirit was, in effect, instinct and personal whim, which, in his terms, became identical with the Divine Imperative, but which, in practice, amounted to a kind of benevolent if not invariably beneficent sentimentalism. The religious experience for Emerson was a kind of good-natured self-indulgence."[8] And then there is the less damning, but in its way perhaps the more cutting, remark of Perry Miller: "Fortunately", speaking of all the transcendentalists, "no one is compelled to take them seriously."[9] But we should take them seriously. After all, in Hawthorne's *The Blithedale Romance* it is the critic of transcendentalism, Miles Coverdale, who is finally the dreamer in his isolating realism. The days at Blithedale turn out to have been, in Jamesian retrospect and recognition, his best.[10]

When we read Emerson we discover a structural and thematic curve and it is just in this circularity, I believe, that the answer to the problem in Emerson is to be found. "Sometimes the world seemed to him to have independent material existence, colored and interpreted by mind", Stuart Brown wrote, "and sometimes it seemed to him wholly dependent and ideal. He never could entirely make up his mind."[11] What I wish to show is that this inconsistency (and all others it implies: time-eternity, subject-object, individual-society) is a logical inconsistency and that

---

5   *The Complete Essays and Other Writings of Ralph Waldo Emerson*, ed. Brooks Atkinson (New York, 1950), 288. Hereafter page references are in the text.
6   "William James and Emerson," 44.
7   New York, 1963, XII, 297.
8   Norfolk, Conn., 1938, 126.
9   "Jonathan Edwards to Emerson", *New England Quarterly*, XIII (1940), 591.
10   "But no – I never can account for it – that, with a yearning interest to learn the upshot of all my story, and returning to Blithedale for that sole purpose, I should examine these things so like a peaceful-bosomed naturalist. Nor why, amid all my sympathies and fears, there shot, at times, a wild exhilaration through my frame!" (Columbus, Ohio, 1964, III, 205). In Coverdale's view the price of idealism is the extinction of reality. But a rejection of that idealism involves him in a cynicism that is perhaps more dehumanizing and dangerous.
11   "Emerson's Platonism", *New England Quarterly*, XVIII (1945), 336.

it stems from his contact with Plato; that Emerson did in fact make up his mind – or imagination – but with a difference, a difference which is one of the more significant philosophic shifts. Briefly: by interpreting Plato, he chose neither spirit nor matter but viewed each as aspects of a ground of being, higher than both. For this reason he is a pragmatist and an idealist without, strictly speaking, being either one. It is his answer to that dilemma posed by George Ripley in the *Dial:* "Spiritualism and materialism both have their foundation in our nature, and both will exist and exert their influence. Shall they exist as antagonist principles? Is the bosom of Humanity to be eternally torn by these two contending factions?... Here then is the mission of the present. We are to reconcile spirit and matter... Nothing else remains for us to do. Stand still we cannot. To go back is equally impossible."[12]

It is important to notice from this statement that Ripley is not advocating idealism, for to advocate one side of the opposition can scarcely be called a reconciliation. If we object that the idealists do not deny the reality of matter, affirming it as a manifestation or phenomenon of spirit, it can be argued that neither do the materialists deny the reality of spirit, affirming it as a development or phenomenon of matter. "Emerson knew only too well", Robert Pollock wrote in *Thought*, "that reality resists every attempt to reduce it to an undifferentiated whole, such as is to be found in a materialistic or spiritualistic monism."[13] The "mission of the present" was to find a third principle under which both could be subsumed. In his essay on Plato, Emerson called it a "union of impossibilities" (479). In view of this I think Charles Feidelson is right when he says that Emerson's originality "consisted in trying to take his stand precisely at the gateway through which these movements pass";[14] "each extreme was tacitly conditioned by a third view in which both became partial".[15]

If we are prone to regard this monistic dualism, or dualistic monism, as a contradiction, then we should keep two things in mind: (1) the question is not so much what do we think now but what did Emerson think then; we must get that straight first; and (2) "contradiction itself", as Stuart

---

[12] Quoted in Charles Feidelson, Jr., *Symbolism and American Literature* (Chicago, 1959), 115.
[13] "A Reappraisal of Emerson", 104.
[14] *Symbolism and American Literature*, 127.
[15] Feidelson, 124.

Brown remarks, "is sometimes only the logical name for mystery".[16]
On the contrary, it seems to me that comparatively recent books – such as
Pierre Teilhard de Chardin's *The Phenomenon of Man* – are stating in
longhand what the gnomic shorthand of Emerson has led us to mis-
construe and therefore reject. George Santayana's statement is probably
correct finally: "If we ask ourselves what was Emerson's relation to the
scientific and religious movements of his time, and what place he may
claim in the history of opinion, we must answer that he belonged very
little to the past, very little to the present, and almost wholly to that
abstract sphere into which mystical or philosophic aspiration has carried
a few men in all ages."[17]

Mystic or philosophic might be one way of putting it, but imaginative
is more precise when applied to Emerson's conclusion, for the conflict
of which monistic dualism is his resolution was the dilemma of the age,
and perhaps Santayana is a little too hasty in removing him from any
historic milieu. We have already seen that milieu typified in Coleridge.
Though the breakthrough made by him is often labeled pantheistic (i.e.
he identified matter with spirit), we saw that his deepest thought rather
implies a mutual harmony of those opposites in a higher third realm where
opposites are perceived as coexisting and united. The tension he states
so well is Emerson's too, as well as his resolution, and we must be careful
not to overstress either balance or reconciliation in Emerson's essays.
The poise he demands is difficult to hold, for while he desires and
emphasizes change and matter in one essay or paragraph, he does not
want them without permanence and spirit; and when he emphasizes
permanence and spirit in another essay or paragraph, there too it is not
without an equal attraction for change and matter. An implicit third
realm always magnetizes both movements. The polarity is between matter
or materialism on the one hand, then, and spirit or idealism on the other.
Unifying them without sacrificing the properties of either is Emerson's
Romantic calculus. Matter is good because it has what spirit lacks and
possesses the desired quality only because it does lack what is associated
with spirit (permanence); and spirit is good because it has what matter
lacks and is good only because it does lack what is associated with
matter (change). We are faced with the dilemma that what makes each
desirable is precisely what makes each inadequate by itself: their opposition to each other. Nevertheless, as Max Deutschbein wrote, "synthesis

---

16   "Emerson's Platonism", 339.
17   *Interpretations of Poetry and Religion* (New York, 1957), 231.

is the fundamental principle of Romanticism; it is its most precious good and its most inner secret".[18]

On the surface it looks like only wishful thinking, having your cake and eating it too, but we begin to think twice when we learn that such a stream of thought was implicit in Plato himself, and that, in fact, almost two thousand years of philosophy – and literature – have in one way or another dealt with the same problem. In "Experience" Emerson wrote, "I know that the world I converse with in the city and in the farms, is not the world I *think*. I observe that difference, and shall observe it. One day I shall know the value and law of this discrepance" (363-364). That day came when Emerson read the *Timaeus*. There he found "the value and law of this discrepance". If the dialogue is grasped then Emerson's seemingly inconsistent position becomes movingly clear.

The essay "Plato; Or, the Philosopher" does swing back and forth between two opposite poles: the one and the many, spirit and matter. Such motion corroborates the content: "If speculation tends thus to a terrific unity, in which all things are absorbed, action tends directly backwards to diversity. The first is the course or gravitation of mind; the second is the power of nature... These two principles reappear and interpenetrate all things, all thought; the one, the many" (477). Here, though, we discover the single reason behind the two principles as we do not in other essays. Emerson found Plato a monistic dualist; he found him believing that spirit and matter have an existence independent of each other, i.e., one is not a refinement of the other, but hinting at a higher ground in which they are reconciled into a dipolar unity. Plato's movement, like Emerson's, is what we saw in Keats's ode: there is permanence (spirit) and there is change (matter); somewhere they gather, although here and now they would seem to cancel each other out. I suggested earlier that this was not just wishful thinking, that the attitude, as Emerson said, is "somewhat better than whim at last". We can now discover why.

In any copy of the *Timaeus* one passage might be set off in capitals or by italic type, for its influence on subsequent thought is nearly incalculable. It is this passage which Emerson chooses to quote; the rest of the essay revolves around it as does Emerson's philosophy itself:

Let us declare the cause which led the Supreme Ordainer to produce and compose the universe. He was good; and he who is good has no kind of envy. Exempt from envy, he wished that all things should be as much as possible

---

[18]   *Das Wesen des Romantischen* (Cöthen, 1921), 2.

like himself. Whosoever, taught by wise men, shall admit this as the prime cause of the origin and foundation of the world, will be in the truth. (480)

If we can unravel that, we can understand Emerson. Luckily, it has already been done for us. Arthur Lovejoy's book *The Great Chain of Being* is entirely devoted to the ramifications of this passage.[19] The explication of Plato, from which his examination proceeds, can be summarized as follows:

(a) If God is perfect then it is impossible that he could be jealous of anything less perfect, but if this is so then

(b) he requires by this necessity of his own nature, by this very perfect completion, that there be things less perfect, less complete, and therefore

(c) the world and its diversity paradoxically complete God, and we are logically faced with an empirical infinity, an absolute immersed in the relative.

This sounds like syntactic high jinks to the modern reader, a sort of verbal abracadabra, but Mr. Lovejoy has demonstrated conclusively the pervasive influence which this ambiguity of "Two-Gods-in-One, of a divine completion which was yet *not* complete in itself", has had down the centuries. Somehow, because of his very completeness, God is incomplete: he requires the world. Since God requires material things, there must be a higher ground of which both matter and spirit are attributes. We can begin to see a pattern to Emerson's apparent inconsistency – shifting back and forth with an emphasis first on spirit and then on matter. Following Plato's speculation he is postulating a third realm beyond both and containing both. Mr. Henry David Gray writes cogently on this point:

just as we are driven from Materialism by the need to take account of the appearance of something forever different from matter, so we are driven from the deeper but still inadequate conception of evolving spirit, in order to give any reality or independence to the individual. And thus is Emerson driven to his final theory of the identity of subject and object in "a substance older and deeper than either mind or matter." ... We must find this Reality to be essentially One, yet to include in itself both spirit and nature, and to have therefore a reality as great as theirs and a potency as effective in producing a world of actual spirit and of actual nature.[20]

---

[19]  The relevant passage is quoted above on 38.
[20]  *Emerson: A Statement of New England Transcendentalism as Expressed in the Philosophy of Its Chief Exponent* (New York, 1970), 51. Cf. this remark of Carl Jung, *Collected Works*, X, 411: "Both views, the materialistic as well as the spiritualistic, are metaphysical prejudices. It accords better with experience to suppose that living matter has a psychic aspect, and the psyche a physical aspect. If we give due con-

This reality, in Emerson's phrase, is "the union of impossibilities" or "the marriage of thoughts and things".

That Emerson saw in Plato what Mr. Lovejoy has shown us is there can not be doubted. First there is the fact that he quoted the same passage, which would not be significant by itself except that Emerson goes on and describes Plato's philosophy in such a way as to prove he did have that passage especially in mind and was fully aware of its implications. The tone of the essay is one of complete approval and affirmation in which Emerson clearly allies himself with the Greek philosopher. In Plato "a balanced soul was born, perceptive of the two elements"; his argument, Emerson tells us, is "self-poised and spherical"; he saw the "upper and the under side of the medal of Jove", and "imbibed the idea of one Deity, in which all things are absorbed. The unity of Asia and the detail of Europe; the infinitude of the Asiatic soul and the defining, result-loving, machine-making, surface-seeking, opera-going Europe – Plato came to join, and, by contact, to enhance the energy of each. The excellence of Europe and Asia are in his brain" (478-479).

There is one remark which urges the polarity we find throughout Emerson and restates what Ripley had called "the mission of the present"; but more than this it develops A and B of the formula above: "All philosophy, of East and West, has the same centripetence. Urged by an opposite necessity, the mind returns from the one to that which is not one, but other or many; from cause to effect; and affirms the necessary existence of variety, the self-existence of both, as each is involved in the other. These strictly-blended elements it is the problem of thought *to separate and to reconcile*" (476, my italics). That is to arrive at C, at a philosophy of dualistic monism, of "Two-Gods-in-One".

Emerson found the same duality in the *Timaeus* and he saw the conjunction that Plato was leading to. In "Works and Days" he calls it a "mid-plain", and we can place special emphasis on the passage in which it occurs, for just previous to it Emerson had written that "the scholar must look for the right hour for Plato's *Timaeus*":

---

sideration to the facts of parapsychology, then the hypothesis of the psychic aspect must be extended beyond the sphere of biochemical processes to matter in general. In that case all reality would be grounded on an as yet unknown substrate possessing material and at the same time psychic qualities. In view of the trend of modern theoretical physics, this assumption should arouse fewer resistances than before."

This miracle is hurled into every beggar's hands. The blue sky is a covering for
a market and for the cherubim and seraphim. The sky is the varnish or glory
with which the Artist has washed the whole work, – the verge or confines of
matter and spirit. Nature could no farther go. Could our happiest dream come
to pass in solid fact, – could a power open our eyes to behold "millions of
spiritual creatures walk the earth," – I believe I should find that mid-plain on
which they move floored beneath and arched above with the same web of blue
depth which weaves itself over me now, as I trudge the streets on my affairs.[21]

Explicit is the dichotomy and the desire for union – not one into the
other but both into a third of "spiritual creatures" and "solid fact";
both into a dualism which is nevertheless monistic, a oneness of two.
That this is what he means is clear from a journal entry on May 26, 1839.
Though he is speaking of man's relationship to nature, this is the vibra-
tion of a higher conclusion to a lower level; the meaning is the same
though the terms are different: "If, as Hedge thinks, I overlook great
facts in stating the absolute laws of the soul; if, as he seems to represent
it, the world is not a dualism, is not a bipolar unity, but is *two*, is Me and
It, then is there the alien, the unknown, and all we have believed and
chanted out of our deep instinctive hope is a pretty dream."[22]

In beginning his book, F. O. Matthiessen rightly says that "the problem
that confronts us in dealing with Emerson is the hardest we shall have to
meet, because of his inveterate habit of stating things in opposites".
Matthiessen goes on to say, however, that the "representative man whom
he most revered was Plato. For Plato had been able to bridge the gap
between the many and the One, society and solitude."[23] Emerson's essay
on Plato seems to me the key to that "inveterate habit of stating things in
opposites". From the apex of the triangle, that "substance older and
deeper than either mind or matter", which Plato implies, Emerson can
look down with equal favor upon ascetic withdrawal and business know-
how, upon the left angle of material progress and upon the right angle
of spiritual development. "A believer in Unity, a seer of Unity, I yet
behold two":[24]

So intimate is this Unity, that, it is easily seen, it lies under the undermost
garment of Nature, and betrays its source in Universal Spirit. (25)

[21]  From *Society and Solitude, The Complete Works of Ralph Waldo Emerson*, ed.
Edward Waldo Emerson (Boston, 1903-1921), VII, 171.
[22]  *Journals of Ralph Waldo Emerson*, ed. Edward Waldo Emerson and Waldo
Emerson Forbes (Boston, 1909-1914), V, 206.
[23]  *American Renaissance*, 3.
[24]  *Journals*, IV, 248.

But

Therefore is Space, and therefore Time, that man may know that things are not huddled and lumped, but sundered and individual. A bell and a plough have each their use, and neither can do the office of the other. Water is good to drink, coal to burn, wool to wear; but wool cannot be drunk, nor water spun, nor coal eaten. The wise man shows his wisdom in separation, in gradation, and his scale of creatures and of merits is as wide as nature. (21)

And so

We live in succession, in division, in parts, in particles. Meantime within man is the soul of the whole; the wise silence; the universal beauty, to which every part and particle is equally related; the eternal One. And this deep power in which we exist and whose beatitude is all accessible to us, is not only self-sufficing and perfect in every hour, but the act of seeing and the thing seen, the seer and the spectacle, the subject and the object, are one. We see the world piece by piece, as the sun, the moon, the animal, the tree; but the whole, of which these are the shining parts, is the soul. (262)

Emerson can sound materialistic in "Self-Reliance" and "Experience" or idealistic in "The Transcendentalist" and "Nature", or he can combine asceticism and worldliness as in "Circles". The simultaneous superiority of action and "what is intellectualized", in James's terms, is possible because both are part and parcel of the same ground; though opposite on the triangle, both lines eventually converge and mingle at the same point. "Each new step we take in thought reconciles twenty seemingly discordant facts, as expressions of one law. Aristotle and Plato are reckoned the respective heads of two schools. A wise man will see that Aristotle platonizes. By going one step farther back in thought, discordant opinions are reconciled by being seen to be two extremes of one principle" (283).

We have started off on the wrong foot with Emerson, or rather on two wrong feet. He is not an idealist. He is not a materialist. He does not dissolve matter into spirit nor does he dismiss spirit into matter. Neither idealists nor materialists have understood the Emersonian principle that only the whole truth could be true at all. The art of Plato, which he describes in very Romantic language, is surely his own as well:

Every great artist has been such by synthesis. Our strength is transitional, alternating; or, shall I say, a thread of two strands. The sea-shore, sea seen from shore, shore seen from sea; the taste of two metals in contact; and our enlarged powers at the approach and at the departure of a friend; the experience of poetic creativeness, which is not found in staying at home, nor yet in travelling, but in transitions from one to the other, which must therefore be adroitly managed to present as much transitional surface as possible; this command of two elements must explain the power and the charm of Plato. (479-480)

In *The Shaping of the Modern Mind*, Crane Brinton speaks of the "eternal contrast, the eternal tension, so strong in Western culture, between this world and the next, the real and the ideal, the practical and the desirable".[25] The tension is especially strong in Emerson. Floyd Stovall's description of the typical American fits him snugly: "His very egotism is heartening because it is naive, as if it were but the measure of his pride in his humanity. Beyond question, he is a materialist; yet in his heart of hearts he is also a perfectionist and an idealist. He who would understand America must resolve this contradiction."[26]

It is true. We keep asking ourselves with Thoreau at Walden, "Shall I go to heaven or a-fishing?"[27] Americans are caught between hating what is not spiritual and loving all that is most delicious of earth. We can not tolerate the tediousness of the world or the effervescence of heaven; so we chase Moby Dick, the great symbol, who can swim, dive, and roll (because in time and in a real ocean), but everlastingly (because in timelessness and spacelessness).

Melville was not so far away from Emerson and Thoreau as he thought he was and as critics have taken him to be. From *Mardi* there is Babbalanja's philosophy, clearly approved, of "things infinite in the finite; and dualities in unities" to belie this. Secondly, and more important, there is Plinlimmon's pamphlet, "Ei", in *Pierre*, interpreted by Mary Dichmann as a summation of Melville's philosophy.[28] The ideas are just those we find in Emerson. One passage from "Ei" reads: "And yet it follows not from this, that God's truth is one thing and man's truth another; but... by their very contradictions they are made to correspond." And further, this passage: "For he will then see, or seem to see, that this world's seeming incompatibility with God, absolutely results from its meridional correspondence with him."[29] Pierre carries the pamphlet in his overcoat all the time unaware that it contains the solution to his problem, caught as he is, like Lycius and Endymion, between the pull of the dark moon and the full, between the poles of realism and idealism.

[25]   New York, 1959, 241.
[26]   *American Idealism* (Norman, Oklahoma, 1943), 4.
[27]   *The Writings of Henry David Thoreau* (New York, 1968), II, 249.
[28]   "Absolutism in Melville's *Pierre*", *PMLA*, LXVII (1952), 702-715.
[29]   New York, 1963, IX, 296-297. Some read Plinlimmon's pamphlet as Melville's satiric portrayal of moral expediency. But for this view there are Melville's own words from *White Jacket* to be reckoned with: "To be efficacious, Virtue must come down from aloft, even as our blessed Redeemer came down to redeem our whole man-of-war world; to that end, mixing with its sailors and sinners as equals" (New York, 1963, VI, 287: the concluding words of Chapter LIV).

Emerson and Melville came to the same solution, the Romantic one, now Americanized: There is no reason for being alarmed that if you choose one, the earth, you automatically lose the other, heaven, and *vice versa;* you can have both, change and permanence, because they are together in a third realm. Emerson did not deny the material any more than Melville denied the spiritual. Both were trying to save each from confiscation by the other. They represent two aspects of the same problem but we forget that they were after the same chiastic conclusion: sea-shore, sea seen from shore, shore seen from sea.

## 2. WALT WHITMAN: THE MIND'S RETURN

> one Whitman is miracle enough, and when he comes again it will be the end of the world.
>
> Randall Jarrell

Hart Crane called Allen Tate to account for decrying the materialism in Whitman without having read *Democratic Vistas*. Except for Crane, I do not know who else besides Kenneth Burke has seen in *Democratic Vistas* a statement of policy that Whitman made personal in *Leaves of Grass*.[30] But Mr. Burke's argument is convincing. The first stage of Democracy for Whitman was the getting down of governing principles. We can call this the stage of thesis, of Spirit. The second stage was the materialization of those principles into creature comforts. This would be the point we are now at, the second part of the dialectic – the antithetical stage of Matter. But Whitman does not stop here – this was Crane's point; it is not a question of well-being for him but of more-being. Yet to come out from the second stage, but beginning, is the final stage where the thesis of Spirit and the antithesis of Matter combine in a synthesis of Spiritualized Matter or Materialized Spirit. The text in question is important enough to Whitman's thought to be given at length:

For the New World, indeed, after two grand stages of preparation-strata, I perceive that now a third stage, being ready for (and without which the other two were useless), with unmistakable signs appears. The First stage was the planning and putting on record the political foundation rights of immense masses of people – indeed all people – in the organization of republican National, State, and municipal governments, all constructed with reference

---

[30] "Policy Made Personal", *"Leaves of Grass" One Hundred Years After*, ed. Milton Hindus (Stanford, 1955).

to each, and each to all. This is the American programme, not for classes, but for universal man, and is embodied in the compacts of the Declaration of Independence... The Second stage relates to material prosperity, wealth, produce, labor-saving machines, iron, cotton, local, State and continental railways, intercommunication and trade with all lands, steamships, mining, general employment, organization of great cities, cheap appliances for comfort, numberless technical schools, books, newspapers, a currency for money circulation, etc. The Third stage, rising out of the previous ones, to make them and all illustrious, I, now, for one, promulge, announcing a native expression-spirit, getting into form, adult, and through mentality, for these States, self-contain'd, different from others, more expansive, more rich and free, to be evidenced by original authors and poets to come, by American personalities, plenty of them, male and female, traversing the States, none excepted – and by native superber tableaux and growths of language, songs, opera, orations, lectures, architecture – and by a sublime and serious Religious Democracy sternly taking command, dissolving the old, sloughing off surfaces, and from its own interior and vital principles, reconstructing, democratizing society.[31]

The policy is poetized when catalogues of things in his poetry are invested with a powerful tone of this futurism. Accordingly, anaphora in his poetry is not simply repetition: he likes things well enough, indeed, but he likes them and repeats them because their completeness heralds a further happening which the etymological sense of anaphora reveals: "act of carrying up, ascent, offering." Indeed, the use of the word by the Eastern church is closest to Whitman's practice: "the portion of the liturgy in which the eucharistic elements are offered as an oblation"; "the eucharistic oblation". All things of earth are offered as harbingers of the true son of God who will come singing his songs. "The good day will come" was inscribed on Shelley's ring, and that is the feeling Whitman's poetry generates. What I wish to show is that this literary good day has other support: the geo-biology of Pierre Teilhard de Chardin and the psychology of Jung clarify this central aspect of Whitman's thought and ground it in possibility – Teilhard would say inevitability.

The following is from Teilhard de Chardin's *The Future of Man*. I quote at length again to assure that the two texts, so important to their respective authors, will be joined in our minds:

The first phase was the formation of proteins up to the stage of the cell. In the second phase individual cellular complexes were formed, up to and including Man. We are now at the beginning of a third phase, the formation of an organico-social super-complex, which, as may easily be demonstrated, *can only occur* in the case of reflective, personalised elements. First the vitalisation of matter,

[31] *Complete Writings*, ed. Richard Bucke, Thomas Harned, Horace Traubel (New York, 1902), V, 123-125.

associated with the grouping of molecules; then the hominisation of Life, associated with a supergrouping of cells; and finally the planetisation of Mankind, associated with a *closed* grouping of people: Mankind, born on this planet and spread over its entire surface, coming gradually to form around its earthly matrix a single, hyper-complex, hyper-centrated, hyper-conscious arch-molecule, co-extensive with the heavenly body on which it was born. Is not this what is happening at the present time – the closing of this spherical, thinking circuit?[32]

Here what Whitman had announced in his essay is given scientific backing. The evolution of life points to just that third stage Whitman envisioned in *Democratic Vistas*. "Passage to India" poetizes this process of evolution; it is a poem about Life, the whole movement and history of life from its beginnings to the present and beyond. The poem is an inference of what is to come out of what has been given. To come is the "closing of this spherical, thinking circuit" and the emergence of an ensemble Mankind out of individual Man with the final development of "the hyper-conscious arch-molecule". For just such reason is importance given in the poem to the Suez canal, the Atlantic cable, and the meeting of railroads – syzygies each of the final synthesis that is beginning, "man's long probation fill'd, / Thou rondure of the World at last accomplish'd". And this "planetisation of Mankind" is responsible for the tone of ecstasy that each hurried verse sounds as it spills the great message. The linkage "Tying the Eastern to the Western Sea, / The road between Europe and Asia" heralds the first glimmer of what Teilhard termed the Noosphere, a layer of mind as the zenith of evolution when physical complexity and sheer plurality are such that psychic unity will be complete and earth will arrive at its Omega point – "the gradual incorporation of the World in the Word Incarnate".[33] So, in the poem "The true son of God shall come singing his songs" and

> All these separations and gaps shall be taken up and hook'd and link'd together,
> The whole earth, this cold, impassive, voiceless earth, shall be completely justified...

By a hundred years Whitman anticipated the theories of Teilhard now affecting scientific and theological circles. His poetry promulgates such a hyper-complex, hyper-centrated network: a criss-crossing of particulars that progressively in their complexity and containment enfold and

[32] Trans. Norman Denny (New York, 1964), 115.
[33] *The Future of Man*, 35.

universalize. The structure of his verse is the structure that Teilhard sees Life and evolution following – greater and greater complexity leading to deeper and deeper integration and unity. "The sense of the earth opening and exploding upwards into God", Teilhard writes, "and the sense of God taking root and finding nourishment downwards into Earth. A personal, transcendent God and an evolving Universe no longer forming two hostile centres of attraction, but entering into hierarchic conjunction to raise the human mass on a single tide. Such is the sublime transformation which we may with justice foresee, and which in fact is beginning to have its effect upon a growing number of minds, free-thinkers as well as believers: the idea of a spiritual evolution of the Universe. The very transformation we have been seeking!"[34]

The double sense of earth opening and God taking root is the sense of Whitman's verse. He foresaw this "sublime transformation" in *Democratic Vistas* which outlines the process and in *Leaves of Grass* which poetizes it. "The critical point of Reflexion in the biological unit becomes the critical point of *In*flexion for the phyla", Teilhard wrote, "which in turn becomes the point of '*circum*flexion'... for the whole sheaf of inward-folding phyla."[35] Whitman reached the critical point of Reflexion in "Song of Myself" and the critical point of Inflexion in *Drum-Taps*, the depiction of masses of men united in mind for a single purpose – "Mannahatta a-march – and it's O to sing it well!" The point of circum-flexion is reached in *Autumn Rivulets*, especially in "Passage to India" where physical complexity and convergence make ready the liberation of the final sphere of mind which is to dovetail with God:

> O soul, repressless, I with thee and thou with me,
> Thy circumnavigation of the world begin,
> Of man, the voyage of his mind's return,
> To reason's early paradise,
> Back, back to wisdom's birth, to innocent intuitions,
> Again with fair creation.

The return is to childlike regions infinitized by absence:

> Whose air I breathe, whose ripples hear, lave me all over,
> Bathe me O God in thee, mounting to thee,
> I and my soul to range in range of thee.

"Passage to India" recounts the three stages of his dialectic: (1) the setting down of principles: "the earth to be spann'd, connected by net-

---

[34]  *The Future of Man*, 80.
[35]  *The Future of Man*, 159.

work"; (2) the realization of those principles: the canal, cable, and rail-roads, "the procession of steamships", "the locomotives rushing and roaring". The "Laramie plains", "the plentiful larkspur and wild onions", "the Wind river and the Wahsatch mountains" of this stage correspond to Teilhard's biosphere. And (3) the synthesis of the first two stages when

> After the seas are all cross'd, (as they seem already cross'd),
> After the great captains and engineers have accomplish'd their work,
> After the noble inventors, after the scientists, the chemist, the geologist,
> > ethnologist,
> Finally shall come the poet worthy of that name,
> The true son of God shall come singing his songs.

The poem shuttles the history, myth, geography, and religion of the past and present together into the future's tapestry. Like the right arms of the four Evangelists in medieval art, all point to a common center, the aureole towards which everything is moving: Omega Point. It is this third state (the Noosphere for Teilhard) for which the other two stages, Whitman said, were only "preparation-strata":

> A worship new I sing,
> You captains, voyagers, explorers, yours,
> You engineers, you architects, machinists, yours,
> You, not for trade or transportation only,
> But in God's name, and for thy sake O soul.

Such was Whitman's vision and such is Teilhard's hypothesis which is based, he insists (like Jung in this respect), upon an interpretation of empirical data: "By interiorising itself under the influence of the Sense of Evolution, planetisation (as the theory of complexity would lead us to expect) can physically have but one effect: it can only personalise us more and more, and eventually (as can be demonstrated by following to their conclusion all the successive stages of its twofold demand for whole-ness and irreversibility) 'divinise' us through access to some Supreme Centre of universal convergence."[36]

Ruling everywhere in Whitman's poetry as the structural equivalent of this theme is the principle of the syzygy which Jung sees the Self in terms of: "the tension of opposites from which the divine child is born as the symbol of unity."[37] The tension is the Romantic one: that between Heaven-Spirit and Earth-Matter. Gebhard Frei, discussing the method

---

[36] *The Future of Man*, 135-136.
[37] *Psyche and Symbol*, ed. Violet S. de Laszlo (New York, 1958), 30.

and teaching of Jung, describes the tension and its desirable resolution: "not to deny or to eliminate matter, but on the one hand to spiritualise matter, and on the other to materialise the spirit by symbolisation."[38] The only way of achieving this ideal is to perceive the Self, for "between the male *Pneuma* (spirit) at the top and the female Matter at the bottom, is *Psyche, separating and also linking* them". When the Psyche is perceived, opposites conjoin because "Matter has not been eliminated or excluded, on the contrary, 'there will be a new heaven and a new earth': spiritualised matter and embodied spirit: *wholeness*."[39] I suggest that Whitman was first torn between these pairs and then perceived in the Self their co-existence and conjunction; that the perception was, in terms of Jungian psychology, a conversion; and that the conversion in turn liberated his poetic powers. His integration of the anima or feminine earth principle through recognition had yielded the complete Self – the *coniunctio* of the masculine and feminine (spirit and matter, heaven and earth). For this reason he hails his soul ("thee of tableaus twain") over and over again everywhere in his poetry. His Psyche, while it gave him the terms of the other two as well, became propaedeutic to the third stage he envisaged outwards by having looked and seen so deeply inward. Teilhard in science today corroborates Whitman's vision outwards, as Jung in psychology does the universality of his perception inward. The Self, Democracy, and the Noosphere are synonymous terms meaning one thing: Spiritu-alized matter or embodied spirit: Incarnation. Both the Noosphere and the composition of the Self merge in these lines from "Passage to India" which point to the fulfillment of Democracy in the picture of earth as mandala:

> Lo, soul, seest thou not God's purpose from the first?
> The earth to be spann'd, connected by network,
> The races, neighbors, to marry and to be given in marriage,
> The oceans to be cross'd, the distant brought near,
> The lands to be welded together.
>
> O vast Rondure, swimming in space,
> Cover'd all over with visible power and beauty,

---

[38] Cf. Whitman's note in "Notes on the Meaning and Intention of *Leaves of Grass*", *Complete Writings*, IX, 3: "Great constituent elements of my poetry – Two, viz.: Materialism – Spirituality – The Intellect, the Esthetic is what is to be the medium of these and to beautify and make serviceable there."
[39] Frei's essay, "On Analytical Psychology", is the appendix to Victor White's book, *God and the Unconscious* (Cleveland, 1961). The material quoted is on pages 261-262 (my italics).

Alternate light and day and the teeming spiritual darkness,
Unspeakable high processions of sun and moon and countless stars above,
Below, the manifold grass and waters, animals, mountains, trees,
With inscrutable purpose, some hidden prophetic intention,
Now first it seems my thought begins to span thee.

The terms of the perception became both the thematics of Whitman's work and its structure – the structure of the syzygy, a tension of opposites hypostatized by the Incarnation which Jung found the Self to represent. When the earth approaches psychic unity, we can remember from Teilhard, its incorporation in the Word Incarnate would begin: "the 'planetization' of humanity presupposes for its proper development not only the contracting of the earth, not only the organizing and condensing of human thought, but also a *third* factor: the rising in our inward horizon of some psychic cosmic centre, some supreme pole of consciousness, towards which all the elementary consciousnesses of the world shall converge and in which they shall be able to love one another: in other words, the rising *of a God*."[40]

Jung's is the psychology, Teilhard's is the science, and Whitman's is the literary arch-voice in America of Romanticism, the movement whose motto is "Give us both". They say in German, French, and English what Nicolas Berdyaev says in Russian, what the Romantic says in any language:

the disciples of abstract monism... introduce such a sharp distinction between the unique, immobile, and absolutely perfect Divinity, on the one hand, and the world of man, movement, historical destiny, tragic conflicts, plurality, and contradiction, on the other; they introduce such an antithesis and make it so impossible to bridge the gap between its poles, that they establish another extreme and unresolvable form of dualism. The only way to escape it is to deny that form of monism which recognizes only the unique and immobile Absolute as truly existing. *Thus every philosophy and form of religious consciousness, which admits both the monistic and the dualist state, surmounts the hopelessness of such a dualism.* It bridges the gap between the two worlds, grasps the significance of plurality, and considers the tragic experience of man and the world in relation to the destiny of the Absolute itself and the interior drama implicit, predetermined, and fulfilled in its depths.[41]

Whitman would have recognized in Jung and Teilhard kindred spirits admitting "both the monistic and the dualist state". Having written

---

[40]  *Hymn of the Universe*, trans. Simon Bartholomew (New York, 1965), 89-90; Teilhard's emphases.
[41]  *The Meaning of History*, trans. George Reavey (Cleveland, 1962), 51. My italics.

"Chanting the Square Deific", Whitman would have concurred in Jung's analysis of the alchemists' search for gold, because it was the gold for which he compounded spirit and matter as heaven and earth to produce.[42] He panned the gold that is Christ-Self. He found the *quaternio*, the *mysterium coniunctionis* characteristic of the Self in which light and shadow, logos and eros, the masculine trinitarian symbol and the fourth feminine principle – respectively, the ideal of spirituality and materialistic earthbound passion – form a syzygial unity-in-duality that to the Romantic is ever Parousia. Keats had written that "'Beauty is truth, truth beauty'", but the meaning is the same: earth and heaven united in a paradise that is both and neither.

Such unity-in-duality removes what has been a thorn in the side of criticism – the Oriental ideas in Whitman's poetry. Malcolm Cowley, for example, sees in the "Song of Myself" a "system of doctrine... more Eastern than Western", and yet "what is extraordinary about this Eastern element is that Whitman... seems to have known little or nothing about Indian philosophy".[43] He didn't have to: the Self is everyone's though the Western mind has split it in half by assigning ascendancy to the intellect. In the East this is not the case; "as the history of Chinese philosophy shows", Jung wrote, "it has never strayed so far from central psychic facts as to lose itself in a one-sided overdevelopment and over-valuation of a single psychic function. Therefore, the Chinese have never failed to recognize the paradoxes and the polarity inherent in what is alive. The opposites always balanced one another – a sign of high culture."[44] Eastern literature seems almost to hoard the secret of the Whole Self it cultivates – in "The Secret of the Golden Flower", for example, or in *The Tibetan Book of the Dead*. But the treasure is in everyone who can still learn to imagine again; "for this is the extraordinary thing", Jung said of "The Secret of the Golden Flower", "it is a living parallel to the course of psychic development in my patients, none of whom is Chinese".[45] The East that Whitman traveled to is the rare Romantic India of mountain-truth and valley-beauty – the Self. For him it was Xanadu. Whitman found the Romantic's treasure in the Self, the

[42]   Relative to "Chanting the Square Deific", see Jung's graphs of the alchemical quaternity: *Collected Works*, XIV, 101-103. I have discussed the psychological ramifications of Teilhard's biology in "The Alchemy of Teilhard", *Continuum*, 7 (1969), 218-220.
[43]   "'Song of Myself' as Inspired Prophecy", *Whitman's "Song of Myself" – Origin, Growth, Meaning*, ed. James E. Miller, Jr. (New York, 1964), 180.
[44]   *Psyche and Symbol*, 306.
[45]   *Psyche and Symbol*, 308.

unity of opposites, for "we are both valley and mountain", Jung wrote, "with respect to the psyche...[46] Furthermore, Jung maintained, "the union of opposites on a higher level of consciousness is not a rational thing, nor is it a matter of will; it is a psychic process of development which expresses itself in symbols".[47] Gebhard Frei and Jung identify the opposites for us as spirit and matter; their balance and union as spiritualized matter or embodied spirit. This is the dialectic Whitman programmed in *Democratic Vistas*. *Leaves of Grass* is our "Secret of the Golden Flower". His rare psychic find led to his poetics; the poetics grew out of the ecstasy which Mr. Cowley describes as "a rapt feeling of union or identity with God (or the Soul, or Mankind, or the Cosmos)".[48] Mankind and the Cosmos bring us back to Teilhard, for the course he sees them following is precisely the course of the Self as Jung describes it: toward embodied spirit, wholeness.

In Jung, Whitman would have found explicated what he meant by the Self; in Teilhard, what he meant by Mankind and the Cosmos. And what he meant was the same in all three cases: the Incarnation; in literature the symbol, the syzygy, "the tension of opposites from which the divine child is born as the symbol of unity". That is the Self for Jung and the course of the universe for Teilhard. Indeed, the corollary that Teilhard draws from his concepts is one that Whitman would have lustily embraced; the language is almost his own: "everything is animated with a flow of Presence and of Love – the spirit which, emanating from the supreme pole of personalisation, fosters and nourishes the mutual affinity of individualities in process of convergence".[49]

The psychology of Jung and the geo-biology of Teilhard de Chardin reinforce the literature of Whitman by clarifying its thematics on the one hand and pointing to structural equivalents on the other. Teilhard can speak for the three of them, because what he discovered in geo-biology Jung found in psychological analysis and Whitman promulgated in poetry: "Thus do I see the New Jerusalem, descending from Heaven and rising from the Earth." Whitman would have understood the consequence of this belief too: "He who speaks these words before the Tribunal of the

---

[46] *Psyche and Symbol*, 312.
[47] *Psyche and Symbol*, 318. See Jung, *Collected Works*, XII, 270-271: "The place or the medium of realization is neither mind nor matter, but that intermediate realm of subtle reality which can only be adequately expressed by the symbol. The symbol is neither abstract nor concrete, neither rational nor irrational, neither real nor unreal. It is always both..."
[48] "'Song of Myself' as Inspired Prophecy", 180.
[49] *The Future of Man*, 60.

Elders will be laughed at and dismissed as a dreamer."[50] Jung never dismissed any dreamer. How could he? He became too aware that like Adam, as Keats put it, the dreamer might awake from his dreaming and find it true.


### 3. WALDEN AS GOD'S DROP

> The way a word does when
> It senses on one side
> A thing and on the other
> A thought; at either side
> It glances and goes deep
> Together...

> Howard Nemerov

As "The Secret of the Golden Flower" offers a parallel to psychic development, *Walden* certainly also parallels the growth of Thoreau. Furthermore, the book is so planned that not only do we follow Thoreau's growth but we are enabled to change as well if we pay attention not only to what he says but to the way he writes and to the way he organizes his book. One index of growth is initially an unexpected one: the extent to which language becomes concrete. In this respect Thoreau does follow Emerson's bold remark, reminiscent of Coleridge, about truth and language:

A man's power to connect his thought with its proper symbol, and so to utter it, depends on the simplicity of his character, that is, upon his love of truth and his desire to communicate it without loss. The corruption of man is followed by the corruption of language... But wise men pierce this rotten diction and fasten words again to visible things; so that picturesque language is at once a commanding certificate that he who employs it is a man in alliance with truth and God... It is the blending of experience with the present action of the mind. It is proper creation. It is the working of the Original Cause through the instruments he has already made.[51]

Throughout *Walden* we watch Thoreau (like Heidegger or Pound in our time) on the trail of such sanctity in his fondness for etymology and word division, particularly of words like *leaf*, in the chapter "Spring", in whose compass "you pass from the lumpish grub in the earth to the airy

---

[50] *The Future of Man*, 23.
[51] From the essay "Nature" in *The Complete Essays and Other Writings*, 17.

and fluttering butterfly".[52] The origin of words reveals a past golden
time from which man has strayed through abstraction – from the Latin
word *abstrahere*, "to draw away".[53] What draws away is the relationship
between the grub and the butterfly, between things and thoughts, and
ultimately the link between the world and God. This occurs first in man
himself when instinct and reason draw apart to form hostile poles in
human nature. Emerson pinpoints the personal time of this occurrence
in the knowledge of our existence; Heidegger pinpoints the collective
time of the breach in Plato's distinction between ideal forms and shadows
in the *Republic*. This is Emerson's remark from "Experience": "It is very
unhappy, but too late to be helped, the discovery we have made that we
exist. That discovery is called the Fall of Man... Once we lived in what
we saw; now, the rapaciousness of this new power, which threatens to
absorb all things, engages us."[54] The new power is reason, and reason by
abstraction tears man from the whole field of being, from the sense of
his being-there and -in. Thoreau goes to Walden to live again in what he
sees and, doing that, to fasten words again to visible things in a proper
creation that is his certificate of a renewed alliance with truth, being, and
God.

The nature of this certificate accounts for the peculiarly Oriental flavor
of *Walden*. Abstraction, in alliance with technology, is a dominate
characteristic of Western man. Symbolization, on the other hand, in
alliance with nature, characterizes classic Eastern thought. In contrast
with abstraction which tears away, symbolization gathers together (from
the Greek word *symballein*, 'to bring together'). Chinese, for example,
gathers the idea to image and image to the idea in the exposed concealedness of the ideograph. Such symbolic language, as Pound believed, is
the exterior sign of man's harmony with himself and with the world he
is in as a creature of the world: the world shows itself in the ideograph
as the vestment or picture of its creatures' ideas. Such a gathering of man
with himself and man with the world is what Thoreau sought in going to
Walden. As he pores over the exposed concealedness of the pond's nature,
the gathering deepens and the language becomes progressively more
imaginative: ideas become more and more inexplicable, not because they
are abstruse, but because they become less and less extricable from the

---

[52] *The Writings of Henry David Thoreau* (New York, 1968), II, 338. Hereafter page
references are in the text.
[53] See Sigmund Freud's review of Karl Abel's pamphlet "The Antithetical Sense of
Primal Words", *Character and Culture*, ed. Philip Rieff (New York, 1963).
[54] *The Complete Essays and Other Writings*, 359.

images they join and which join them. We are given, then, a linguistic
echo of, and way to, the sense of man as a being-in-nature which Thoreau
attains when "every little pine needle expanded and swelled with sympathy", and when he is "made aware of the presence of something
kindred... even in scenes which we are accustomed to call wild" (146).

When we hear of Thoreau's higher laws we must take them with a large
dose of brute fact and of Eastern thought in order to counter the settled
impression of someone leaving the world behind in a vaguely ascetic
thrust to the infinite. He tells us that he "loved so well the philosophy
of India" (67). That philosophy pervades the book directly in quotations
and indirectly in Thoreau's own way of thinking and writing. In the conclusion of chapter sixteen, "The Pond in Winter", Thoreau is explicit
about its importance to him and therefore to us for an understanding
of his thought:

In the morning I bathe my intellect in the stupendous and cosmogonal philosophy
of the Bhagvat-Geeta, since whose composition years of the gods have elapsed,
and in comparison with which our modern world and its literature seem puny
and trivial; and I doubt if that philosophy is not to be referred to a previous
state of existence, so remote is its sublimity from our conceptions. I lay down
the book and go to my well for water, and lo! there I meet the servant of the
Bramin, priest of Brahma and Vishnu and Indra, who still sits in his temple on
the Ganges reading the Vedas, or dwells at the root of a tree with his crust and
water jug. I meet his servant come to draw water for his master, and our buckets
as it were grate together in the same well. The pure Walden water is mingled
with the sacred water of the Ganges. (328-329)

One thing this philosophy of India is not, first of all, is other-worldly.
"Talk of Heaven!" Thoreau says, "ye disgrace earth" (222). "Instead of
calling on some scholar", he writes, "I paid many a visit to particular
trees..." (223). It is a realometer he wants us to have (109) and not an
idealometer.[55] Yet of course Thoreau does urge us to a higher life. Still,
this higher life seems coincident with the life around him. Somewhat
impishly but subtly, he says that only heaven knew why he raised beans
(171). Such relationship between the spiritual and the material is the
treasure Walden holds in its depths – presented, for example, as the old

---

[55]   Cf. Emerson, "Nature", *The Complete Essays and Other Writings*, 32: "The first
and last lesson of religion is, 'The things that are seen, are temporal; the things that
are unseen, are eternal.' It puts an affront upon nature... The uniform language that
may be heard in the churches of the most ignorant sects is – 'Contemn the unsubstantial
shows of the world; they are vanities, dreams, shadows, unrealities; seek the realities
of religion.' The devotee flouts nature."

log canoe or the iron chest. His poem to Walden recalls Emerson's
"Brahma":

> I cannot come nearer to God and Heaven
> Than I live to Walden even.
> I am its stony shore,
> And the breeze that passes o'er...        (215)

The pond is the temple of his philosophy and its shores and surface are the
frieze of his inquiry and adoration. It is decorated by the ground-nut and
a bean-field. It is surrounded by minor deities which Thoreau sculpts with
the naturalist's care and the priest's power – the hoot-owl, the loon, the
pickerel, and the partridge. And these are as apropos for Thoreau's
purpose as the elephant caryatids on the Shiva temples in India. The
iconology is American but the content is Indian. The initiate to the book
*Walden* is meant to learn through patient and long immersion in the text
what the Indian novice sets out to discover through contemplation of the
pictorial *Island of Jewels:*

What is mortal in himself and what is imperishable he should know to be one.
What is changing and what is above change he should discover to be coincident.
Thus he should learn at last to accept the Maya of his transient, frail existence
as a dynamic radiation of the Self-Eternal.[56]

It is an Eastern – and Romantic – lesson, for the transcendence suggested
is not of conflict itself, but of the logic which says that conflict or contradiction can not continue within unity. The transcendence is of polar
coexistence alone to coexistence within existence itself.

Thoreau does not let us wander from all the ramifications of such
harmony between what is changing and what is above change. He starts
with action and contemplation. In "Economy", he asks, "Is it impossible
to combine the hardiness of these savages with the intellectualness of the
civilized man?" (14) And in "Higher Laws", again, he remarks: "I found
in myself, and still find, an instinct toward a higher, or, as it is named,
spiritual life, as do most men, and another toward a primitive rank and
savage one, and I reverence them both" (232). The bean-field too is not
spared from the gathering dictated by the pond: "Mine was, as it were,
the connecting link between wild and cultivated fields; as some states are
civilized, and others half-civilized, and others savage or barbarous, so
my field was, though not in a bad sense, a half-cultivated field" (174).

---

[56] Heinrich Zimmer, *Myths and Symbols in Indian Art and Civilization*, ed. Joseph
Campbell (New York, 1962), 210. Cf. Emerson, "Plato; Or the Philosopher", *The
Complete Essays and Other Writings*, 476-477.

The ideally real man comes to be conceived by Thoreau as "but partially risen out of the earth, something more than erect, like swallows alighted and walking on the ground:

> 'And as he spake, his wings would now and then
> Spread, as he meant to fly, then close again'..."          (182)

Just so, whenever Thoreau spreads his wings, he as quickly folds them. If he preaches to us, he as soon describes for us because with Whitman and Emerson he knows that "the lover of nature is he whose inward and outward senses are still truly adjusted to each other; who has retained the spirit of infancy even into the era of manhood. His intercourse with heaven and earth becomes part of his daily food."[57] Having us look up in "Higher Laws" (chapter eleven), he has us immediately look down in "Brute Neighbors" (chapter twelve), for the whole truth for him is neither God nor the world but God in the world and the world in God.

The center of this concurrence is Walden pond itself whose "line of greatest length intersected the line of greatest breadth *exactly* at the point of greatest depth..." (319). The convergence of two opposite lines onto the single point of greatest depth suggests Schelling's idea of God as a harmony of two conflicting modes of action – a fact, he said, "that could not escape the first man who felt and perceived intimately".[58] Thoreau became that first man, and in the central (or deepest) chapter of *Walden*, chapter nine, "The Ponds", Thoreau refers to Walden as "God's Drop". Here, though, the influence is not German but Indian. The passage is this:

The engineer does not forget at night, or his nature does not, that he has beheld this vision of serenity and purity once at least during the day. Though seen but once, it helps to wash out State Street and the engine's soot. One proposes that it be called "God's Drop." (215)

One does not like to write of hidden meanings in Thoreau, since truth in its original sense of unhiddenness *(a-letheia)* is so much the foundation of *Walden*.[59] Still, there is a hidden meaning in the passage, hidden at least to anyone unacquainted with the Hindu concept of the Bindu. And if this is understood one can see that Thoreau intends much more than an

---

[57]  Emerson, "Nature", *The Complete Essays and Other Writings*, 6.
[58]  *The Ages of the World*, 97.
[59]  As shown, for example, in this passage from "Where I Lived, and What I Lived For", *Walden*, 107-108: "Men esteem truth remote, in the outskirts of the system, behind the farthest star, before Adam and after the last man. In eternity there is indeed something true and sublime. But all these times and places and occasions are now

analogous reference to eyewash. Indeed, the phrase placed so carefully in the center of his work shows not only that Thoreau considered the pond as an object for meditation but that he recreated the nature of that object in the structure of his whole work for the reader's own meditation. He would tell us what he learned but more subtly and effectively he would have us learn with him. The following is from Heinrich Zimmer's book *Myths and Symbols in Indian Art and Civilization*. The quotation establishes the importance of Thoreau's apparently casual description. These words are from chapter four, "The Cosmic Delight of Shiva", section three, "Shiva-Shakti":

The Absolute is to be visualized by the concentrating devotee as a vanishing point or dot, "the drop" *(bindu)*, amidst the interplay of all the triangles. This Bindu is the power-point, the invisible, elusive center from which the entire diagram expands.[60]

The Bindu is the central point of the Shri Yantra or the "Yantra above Yantras" which is the highest object of Hindu meditation and prayer. Like Walden, the figure has "no visible inlet nor outlet" (215). The dot or drop, like Walden's greatest depth, is also "in the centre of the map" (319). The yantra, Zimmer explains, "is conceived and designed as a support to meditation – more precisely, to a concentrated visualization and intimate inner experience of the polar play and logic-shattering paradox of eternity and time".[61] It serves as "a representation of some personification or aspect of the divine" and as "a kind of chart or schedule for the gradual evolution of a vision, while identifying the Self with its slowly varying contents, that is to say, with the divinity in all its phases of transformation".[62] The dot or drop is the point on which the Hindu fixes his gaze to identify with God who is visualized as the meeting of the opposite movements of withdrawal and creation portrayed as an interlocking series of expanding and/or diminishing triangles. One series points upward and the other series points downward. The drop where they meet is God's essence and the Self's identity – neither down (i.e., earthly, concrete, finite, individual) nor up (i.e., heavenly, abstract, infinite,

---

and here. God himself culminates in the present moment, and will never be more divine in the lapse of all the ages. And we are enabled to apprehend at all what is sublime and noble only by the perpetual instilling and drenching of the reality that surrounds us." These words about truth as related to God's simultaneous presence in eternity and time prepare for what is capsulate in the phrase under discussion.

[60] Zimmer, 147.
[61] Zimmer, 140.
[62] Zimmer, 141.

**Shrí-Yantra**

universal) but both: what Zimmer calls "the supernal non-dual duality".

Another description of the pond by Thoreau in the same chapter confirms this parallel which enables us to plumb more exactly the depth of his thought and method. "Walden", he writes, "is blue at one time and green at another, even from the same point of view. Lying between the earth and the heavens, it partakes of the color of both" (196). One can object that this is simply careful observation and not covert theology. But it seems to be the genius of Thoreau to make what he sees and describes honestly coincide with what he thinks and believes. He loosens the potency of the actual. This is surely the case here. For him the pond is the pond – no doubt about that; but it also represents the divine which transcends opposites by including them. Thoreau is therefore its concentrating devotee. His transcendentalism is not a matter of going beyond the world but of bridging the gap between this-worldliness and otherworldliness. How successful his long gaze into the pattern of Walden was is clear in these words which show his identification with the slowly varying contents of his vision:

It was very queer, especially in dark nights, when your thoughts had wandered to vast and cosmogonal themes in other spheres, to feel this faint jerk, which came to interrupt your dreams and link you to Nature again. It seemed as if I might next cast my line upward into the air, as well as downward into this element, which was scarcely more dense. Thus I caught two fishes as it were with one hook. (194-195)

Two fishes on one hook is more winning than Zimmer's mind-bogging phrase "non-dual duality", but the content is the same: "Heaven is under our feet as well as over our heads" (313).

The phrase "God's Drop", therefore, suggests that Thoreau planned *Walden* to be a yantra, a chart for the gradual evolution of this vision of God and the Self. He invites the reader to follow and repeat his experience of the pond as an object of meditation: to move down through the first half of the book in the detail of "Economy" and up in the second half to the suggestiveness of "Higher Laws" in order to see that between them in "The Ponds" is the whole truth which partakes of the colors of both the material and the spiritual. Walden was for him and can become for us as the book what the still point also is in the turning world of T. S. Eliot: "Neither flesh nor fleshless; / Neither from nor towards; at the still point, there the dance is."[63]

### 4. A LETTER, – THE LETTER A: NATHANIEL HAWTHORNE

When the familiar scene is suddenly strange
Or the well known is what we have yet to learn,
And two worlds meet, and intersect, and change;

T. S. Eliot

As theology and literature become more and more complementary in theory and analysis, the works of Hawthorne stand out for their cross-fertilization of aesthetic and religious concerns. Hawthorne developed a theory and a way of writing to accord with what he believed about Christianity and about the way human nature develops morally. To do this, in the parlance of the time, was to cultivate the faculty of the

[63] From "Burnt Norton", *Collected Poems 1909-1962* (New York, 1963), 177.

imagination which reconciles disparates into new wholes. Virtually his entire fiction demonstrates what happens when any one person fails to cultivate this faculty. *The Marble Faun*, his final novel, leaves us with a point of reference with which to determine his characters' imaginative achievement. This is the Pantheon in chapter fifty, "that great circle... formerly dedicated to heathen gods, but Christianized through twelve centuries gone by".[64] It "stands almost at the central point of the labyrinthine intricacies" of Rome.[65] It stands in other words, almost at the center of the center of Western culture whose labyrinthine intricacies Hawthorne's works carefully thread. Kenyon's description of the building directs our attention to the double nature of this single structure which bridges heathenism and Christianity. The ritualistic choreography of meaning and emotion in his words seems to stymie any logical comprehension of the building. Like the scarlet letter, this related mystic symbol also evades the mind's analysis but subtly communicates itself to the imagination:

"I think," said the sculptor, "it is to the aperture in the Dome – that great Eye, gazing heavenward – that the Pantheon owes the peculiarity of its effect. It is so heathenish, as it were; – so unlike all the snugness of our modern civilization! Look, too, at the pavement directly beneath the open space! So much rain has fallen there, in the last two thousand years, that it is green with small, fine moss, such as grows over tombstones in a damp English churchyard."[66]

The Pantheon transcends patterned opposites by including both the blue sky above and the green moss below in one architectural harmony. The dictum embodied is that the way up is the way down: the spiritual and the material, intelligence and instinct, are part and parcel of human nature and neither can be denied if the one human life is to be lived with psychological harmony. Analogically, to achieve such a continuum is to travel in a circle. Miriam makes this clear in her depiction of Donatello's career. What she says for this one character restates what the "great circle" of the Pantheon means in another way for all of Hawthorne's characters:

"Is he not beautiful?" said Miriam, watching the sculptor's eye as it dwelt admiringly on Donatello. "So changed, yet still, in a deeper sense, so much the same! He has travelled in a circle, as all things heavenly and earthly do, and now comes back to his original self, with an inestimable treasure of improvement won from an experience of pain."[67]

[64]  *The Marble Faun* (Columbus, Ohio, 1968), IV, 456-457.
[65]  *The Marble Faun*, 456.
[66]  *The Marble Faun*, 457.
[67]  *The Marble Faun*, 434. The symbolism of the circle is reinforced by references to

Painting and sculpture are also used frequently throughout his works to reinforce and expand the analogies in the direction of reconciliation. Since Hawthorne himself saw an exemplary relationship between the white, blank page and added colorful description leading to the finished work, he quotes approvingly Thorvaldsen's parallel between "the Clay-model, the Life; the Plaster-cast, the Death; and the sculptured Marble, the Resurrection",[68] and prefers Perugino to Raphael because the Virgin "revealed herself to him in loftier and sweeter faces of celestial woman-hood, (and yet with a kind of homeliness in their human mould)..."[69] Hawthorne will have neither an essential nor an existential art. The art he prefers, and practices himself, must neither become bogged down in detail to the exclusion of meaning – this would err against the dome of the Pantheon and the soul of man – nor simply use detail as mirrors for meaning – for this would equally err against the floor of the Pantheon and the body of man. The art he prefers and practices as a faithful imitation of the imagination and of the whole man is incarnational in form. An essentialist herself, this is the art which Hilda, in *The Marble Faun*, feels "a vast and weary longing" to see.[70] In this particular passage such form is directly related to the subject:

She never found just the Virgin Mother whom she needed. Here, it was an earthly mother, worshipping the earthly baby in her lap, as any and every mother does from Eve's time downward. In another picture, there was a dim sense, shown in the mother's face, of some divine quality in the child. In a third, the artist seemed to have had a higher perception, and had striven hard to shadow out the Virgin's joy at bringing the Saviour into the world, and her awe and love, inextricably mingled, of the little form which she pressed against her bosom. So far was good. But still, Hilda looked for something more; a face of celestial beauty, but human as well as heavenly, and with the shadow of past grief upon it; bright with immortal youth, yet matronly and motherly, and endowed with a queenly dignity, but infinitely tender, as the highest and deepest attribute of her divinity.[71]

---

the number seven in the novel (the seven-branched Hebrew candlestick and the seven-gemed Etruscan bracelet) which has the same content of the desired whole (as 7) which gathers innocence (3) and experience (4) mysteriously together in the lost candlestick – lost to the modern sensibility – and the antique bracelet. The cherished number in turn is reinforced by grape imagery: on the vine (in Eden), crushed (in the Fall), and made into wine (in the redemption).

[68]  *The Marble Faun*, 380.
[69]  *The Marble Faun*, 339.
[70]  *Ibid.*
[71]  *The Marble Faun*, 348. Cf. *The Scarlet Letter* (Columbus, Ohio, 1962), I, 56: "Had there been a Papist among the crowd of Puritans, he might have seen in this beautiful woman, so picturesque in her attire and mien, and with the infant at her

Similarly, as innocence and experience interact in and between his characters to suggest a mature third view, Hawthorne's own allegorical juxtapositions tend to fade and convert into symbolism. This aesthetic-religious energy of imaginative conversion seems responsible in great measure for the American Renaissance. At the head of that five year period stands *The Scarlet Letter* (1850) where literature and theology are used to clarify each other – first in the theory of "The Custom-House" and then in the fiction itself. In both Pearl is the significant factor.

Hawthorne referred to himself as "a tolerably good Surveyor of the Customs". He does linger a great while in the second storey of the custom-house, poking and burrowing and finally uncovering something whose content is quite foreign and mysterious – the red letter:

This rag of scarlet cloth, – for time, and wear, and a sacrilegious moth, had reduced it to little other than a rag, – on careful examination, assumed the shape of a letter. It was the capital letter A. By an accurate measurement, each limb proved to be precisely three inches and a quarter in length. It had been intended, there could be no doubt, as an ornamental article of dress; but how it was to be worn, or what rank, honor, and dignity, in by-past times, were signified by it, was a riddle which (so evanescent are the fashions of the world in these particulars) I saw little hope of solving. And yet it strangely interested me. My eyes fastened themselves upon the old scarlet letter, and would not be turned aside. Certainly, there was some deep meaning in it, most worthy of interpretation, and which, as it were, streamed forth from the mystic symbol, subtly communicating itself to my sensibilities, but evading the analysis of my mind. (31)

The lines demonstrate the almost comic inadequacy of scientifically aggressive knowing. The pose reminds us of Coverdale in his leafy her-mitage, in *The Blithedale Romance*, looking down and trying to decipher the lives below him. The rag of scarlet cloth elicits a kind of response which defines its own imaginative content by contrast. If our civilization has "yet to learn again the forgotten art of gayety" (232), it has yet as well to learn again the forgotten art of intuition. Hawthorne's "careful examination" of the "riddle" produces the dead fact that by "accurate

---

bosom, an object to remind him of the image of Divine Maternity, which so many illustrious painters have vied with one another to represent; something which should remind him, indeed, but only by contrast, of that sacred image of sinless motherhood, whose infant was to redeem the world. Here, there was the taint of deepest sin in the most sacred quality of human life, working such effect, that the world was only the darker for this woman's beauty, and the more lost for the infant that she had borne." Page references to *The Scarlet Letter* in the text are from this edition.

measurement" "the capital letter A" is "precisely three inches and a quarter in length". The letter is virtually impervious to such an attack. It will not be solved because it is not a problem; it is a mystery – and the sense for mystery is exactly what is lacking in the Surveyor. The voice Hawthorne uses is deliberately assumed to intone the psychological distance between the Puritan past of the letter and the present of narration. The division between intelligence and instinct in the past which the novel treats is no longer even a division: instinct and intuition have simply disappeared altogether. Still, such an intelligence originated with a view which set instinct and reason at war in the first place: out of a religion's one-sided emphasis on rationality and law came this passionless approach to reality. Such an approach suggests that the narrator, Hawthorne, will be directly involved throughout the novel in an examination of the division which led ineluctably to such a sterile pose. And in the process of telling the story of the frayed letter he will uncover its rich and whole meaning for himself and for the American mind as he learns to rest in the mystery of its wide compass – as he turns, that is, from an attitude of analysis to an attitude of receptivity. Continuing to examine the letter, he finally confesses that though his mind is stymied his eyes nevertheless "fastened themselves upon the old scarlet letter, and would not be turned aside". Such wise passiveness yields results; deep meaning "streamed forth from the mystic symbol, subtly communicating itself to my sensibilities, but evading the analysis of my mind". The entire passage in which Hawthorne tries to comprehend the letter insinuates the qualitative difference which Emerson made explicit in *Nature* between the Understanding which "adds, divides, combines, measures", and the Reason which "marries Matter and Mind".[72] Reason is the imagination, the symbol-making faculty which expresses the wholeness of man – mind and body, spirit and matter. Resistant to understanding, the letter appeals to the imagination which must be quickened if the narrator is to possess the letter in its entirety, and it is apparently urgent for him to do so.

Hawthorne uses the deserted parlour in the Old Manse to visualize that quickening (35-36). The imagination is most likely to act, he says, at a time late at night with moonlight falling in the familiar room. He looks about him and the details he sees form a picture which leaves a whole impression though each object has a life of its own. He insists on the multiplicity and unity of the scene. Each object retains its solidity and its individuality – emphasized by the phrases "so completely seen"

---

[72]  *The Complete Essays and Other Writings*, 20.

and "so minutely visible" – and yet the chairs, the centre-table, the sofa, a volume or two are "spiritualized by the unusual light". The objects in the parlour are as distinct as they are during the day but in the light of the moon they are now malleable; new wholes can be formed with no attenuation of any object's discreteness: details are "completely seen" and still "seem to lose their actual substance, and become things of intellect". In the context of the entire passage both "things" and "intellect" carry equal weight: the material remains the material (things stay things) even as it becomes spiritual. Like Donatello, these things are "so changed, yet still, in a deeper sense, so much the same". They have traveled in the circle of the imagination which reveals itself in such distinction without division. The Aristotelian or Thomistic phrase "actual substance" and the word "spiritualized" also give this artistic resolution a theological dimension: they strongly suggest the religious ritual of consubstantiation in which for the faithful the bread and wine, without ceasing to be bread and wine, also become Christ.[73] "Nothing is too small or too trifling to undergo this change, and acquire dignity thereby." Because this sentence refers to the list of his daughter's playthings (a doll, a carriage, a hobby-horse), we sense the inchoate presence of the redemptive motif which Pearl in the novel will come to have for her parents, and that furthermore will continue to be closely paralleled with the creative process from which it initially sprang – the process which harmonizes yet permits individuality. This very domestic but carefully ordered scene where things are "invested with a quality of strangeness and remoteness, though still almost as vividly present as by daylight" has therefore given Hawthorne a way to write which is also attuned to what he will write.

The link between the moral issue of the novel and the creative issue of the introduction is more than intimated in the visual example Hawthorne

---

[73] We can remember that Coleridge gave the imagination such a theological dimension when he described the symbols in the Scriptures as "consubstantial with the truths of which they are the conductors". His definition of the symbol as "the translucence of the eternal through and in the temporal" accords exactly with the way Hawthorne speaks of any kind of art which suits his preference. His characters tend to fall on either side of these values and work towards a center where the eternal and temporal form a continuum. Arthur is "the man of ethereal attributes" (142) – an eternal character; Hester is the woman who "had in her nature a rich, voluptuous, Oriental characteristic, – a taste for the gorgeously beautiful" (83) – a temporal character; Pearl is the visible tie, "the living hieroglyphic" (207) which unites the characteristics of her parents as idea in image. Appropriately, she reminds Mr. Wilson of stained glass, i.e., the translucence of the eternal through and in the temporal.

uses to conclude and illustrate what has been happening in his mind as he sat looking in the parlour. The analogy makes his ideas flesh:

The somewhat dim coal-fire has an essential influence in producing the effect which I would describe. It throws its unobtrusive tinge throughout the room, with a faint ruddiness upon the walls and ceiling, and a reflected gleam from the polish of the furniture. This warmer light mingles itself with the cold spirituality of the moonbeams, and communicates, as it were, a heart and sensibilities of human tenderness to the forms which fancy summons up. It converts them from snow-images into men and women. Glancing at the looking-glass, we behold – deep within its haunted verge – the smouldering glow of the half-extinguished anthracite, the white moonbeams on the floor, and a repetition of all the gleam and shadow of the picture, with one remove farther from the actual, and nearer to the imaginative.

Theoretically the novel is complete here. The picture is a cartoon for the larger canvas to come in the work where the dualistic viewpoint of Puritanism will create clear and distinct contrasts and oppositions to be mingled and converted into a whole view. The full significance of the passage can be illustrated through juxtaposing the positions of Irving Babbitt and Hugh Fausset on the nature of Romantic literature vis-à-vis a theological position. Babbitt insists that Romanticism ignores or confuses what for him is the deep cleft which genuine religion reveals between man's ordinary self and the divine. Hawthorne's approach is similarly dualistic, but only initially: the haunted verge is a third term. Fausset's reply to Babbitt's critical and allegorical Puritanism states explicitly what the passage from Hawthorne implies as creative theory moved naturally on its own terms onto a moral plane: "such an interpretation of Jesus' teaching robbed it of its central revelation, reimposing the very dualism which he convincingly resolved. And not only the earlier, but the sounder tradition of the Church, emphasized the truth that the material and the instinctive are not necessarily divided by a deep cleft from the divine, that the ascetic, whether as medieval monk or Puritan moralist, destroyed life's sacramental wholeness no less than the sensualist... The truest Christian tradition... has discriminated between the natural and the spiritual, but its ideal has been to harmonize them."[74] Hawthorne discriminates between the coal-fire and the moonbeams, which clearly have the connotations of the natural and the spiritual, but he harmonizes them as well in the looking-glass. Hawthorne writing about literature sounds in part like a theologian with words like "spirituality" and "converts", and Fausset writing about theology sounds like

[74]  *The Proving of Psyche* (New York, 1929), 261.

an artist with words like "discriminated" and "harmonize". The two passages might almost be transposed with little or nothing lost. This is not accidental: there is a connection between the nature of art and the nature of religion, and it is that connection which Hawthorne is surely intimating. It is a connection which actually forms the foundation of his novel where a view of art closely resembles a view of religion: both are to bind and bring together.

Many passages confirm in the fiction what had been adumbrated in theory. The following is from Chapter XII, "The Minister's Vigil":

But, before Mr. Dimmesdale had done speaking, a light gleamed far and wide over all the muffled sky... It showed the familiar scene of the street, with the distinctness of mid-day, but also with the awfulness that is always imparted to familiar objects by an unaccustomed light. The wooden houses, with their jutting stories and quaint gable-peaks; the doorsteps and thresholds, with the early grass springing up about them; the garden-plots, black with freshly turned earth; the wheel-track, little worn, and, even in the marketplace, margined with green on either side; – all were visible, but with a singularity of aspect that seemed to give another moral interpretation to the things of this world than they had ever borne before. (153-154)

The personal details of the parlour have been metamorphosed into the public details of the town. We remember the earlier passage: the sofa, the bookcase, and other articles are "invested with a quality of strangeness and remoteness, though still almost as vividly present as by daylight". Now the scene is larger and the application more universal: "It showed the familiar scene of the street, with the distinctness of mid-day, but also with the awfulness that is always imparted to familiar objects by an unaccustomed light." The scene again is well framed, 'margined', very detailed but also bathed in light. This keeps the dimension of art well in the reader's mind as he now is led more to ponder the human anguish of Arthur and Hester. The different moral interpretation accrues from the fact that details and light work not in opposition to each other but together to create an harmonious whole.[75] The wooden houses the

---

[75] The link between the moral and artistic interpretations in Hawthorne's novel forms the basis of a similar 'high argument' – William Wordsworth's. The sexual analogy is clear in these lines from "The Recluse":

How exquisitely the individual Mind
(And the progressive powers perhaps no less
Of the whole species) to the external World
Is fitted: – and how exquisitely, too –
Theme this but little heard of among men –

garden-plots, and all evidence of human activity seem to be sanctified by light. Where Hawthorne went on to infer a definition of the romance from what he had observed in the parlour, this passage concludes with his three main characters instead. Their relationship is therefore very much that of moonbeams and coal-fire to looking-glass: "And there stood the minister, with his hand over his heart; and Hester Prynne, with the embroidered letter glimmering on her bosom; and little Pearl, herself a symbol, and the connecting link between those two."

Hawthorne never tires of alluding to Pearl as a connecting link, a symbol. The context shows that he is using the word in the very exact sense visualized more perfectly in the German word *Sinnbild*, one un-divided word with two distinct natures: *Sinn*, which denotes meaning and idea – by extension, intelligence, the spiritual, and the infinite; *bild*, which denotes picture or image – instinct, the material, and the finite. It is no wonder that Romantic theories of the imagination – Hawthorne's included – quickly acquire religiosity. Other examples confirm this exactitude and direction. When Hester tries to account for Pearl's character, she recalls what she herself had been "while Pearl was im-bibing her soul from the spiritual world, and her bodily frame from its material of earth" (91). She thinks of Pearl "as a spirit-messenger no less than an earthly child" (180). Transcendent of heaven and earth, Pearl is worthy "to be the plaything of the angels" (90), but she mixes with Indians and mariners who are conscious that her nature is wilder than theirs (244-245). It is no surprise that Mr. Wilson asks her whether she is "a Christian child" or "one of those naughty elfs" (110). Pearl comprehends the full scope of opposite impressions because the truth of her nature is the saving relationship between them. The narrator's own words indicate how personally involved he is in the character of Pearl. She has made him travel in a circle: "And Pearl was the oneness of their being. Be the foregone evil what it might, how could they doubt that their earthly lives and future destinies were conjoined, when they beheld at once the material union, and the spiritual idea, in whom they met, and were to dwell immortally together?" (207). Being spiritual and

---

The external World is fitted to the Mind;
And the creation (by no lower name
Can it be called) which they with blended might
Accomplish: – this is our high argument. (ll. 816-824)

In Puritan America, where the town and the wilderness have but an uneasy truce, the sexual analogy in which mind and world fit to create a visible tie between them is adulterous.

material, and yet "the oneness of their being", Pearl is very much as theologians say of Christ, *unus ex duobus*. As serious as the fall of her parents might have been, it is a happy one nevertheless – and for Hawthorne as an artist as well because the echo from "The Custom-House" is also striking. Hester and Arthur will dwell immortally together in the novel too, for the material union and the spiritual idea conjoined is the neutral territory of art which Pearl is also made to be. In her, sacramental overtones meet and mingle naturally with the artist's purpose of reconciling spirit and matter. His too is an incarnational act.[76] The only thing like Pearl is her own reflection in the pool which she understandably flirts with (177, 208): it is her looking-glass. She even creates what she is: "The spell of life went forth from her ever creative spirit, and communicated itself to a thousand objects, as a torch kindles a flame wherever it may be applied. The unlikeliest materials, a stick, a bunch of rags, a flower, were the puppets of Pearl's witchcraft, and, without undergoing any outward change, became spiritually adapted to whatever drama occupied the stage of her inner world" (95). A new moral interpretation, nothing less than the revelation of the truest Christian tradition, is indeed given to the things of this world, an interpretation reinforced by artistic creation.

Mr. Wilson, the Puritan clergyman who embodies one aspect of the pervasive division Hawthorne scrutinizes – his geniality "had been less carefully developed than his intellectual gifts" (65) – can not understand such an interpretation because for one reason he has left behind in the old world the kind of art which is its manifestation. Characteristically looking "like the darkly engraved portraits which we see prefixed to old volumes of sermons" (65), he can only dimly guess Pearl's new covenant and art: "Methinks I have seen just such figures, when the sun has been shining through a richly painted window, and tracing out the golden and crimson images across the floor. But that was in the old land" (109-110). Of course the analogy is playfully grandiose flattery, apt and natural. Still, the terms are variants of those Hawthorne used when he confirmed the old world's right reading of human nature on his own pulse through the common objects of living in his parlour: "Thus, therefore, the floor of our familiar room has become a neutral territory,

---

[76] Cf. William Lynch, *Christ and Apollo*, 158: "It is no small wonder that it is in Christ we come to the fullest possible understanding of what analogy means in the fullest concrete, the facing relentlessly into the two poles of the same and the different and the interpenetrating reconciliation of the two contraries. He who is the Lord of all things is the lord of the imagination."

somewhere between the real world and fairyland, where the Actual and the Imaginary may meet, and each imbue itself with the nature of the other" (36). Mr. Wilson remembers a floor too, a floor on which through its art of stained glass a different Church's point of view is made manifest.[77] On this floor, like the Pantheon's, heaven's light and earth's stain meet and imbue themselves with the nature of the other in an artistic partaking and re-creation of the hypostatic nature of the Christ child. The floor of the church, like the floor of the parlour, is an artistic zone, with now strongly sacramental content, where the spiritual and the material draw together. Certainly Pearl is the mystic symbol in its living form (102).

The community is intrigued with Pearl as much as Mr. Wilson is. And why shouldn't it be where the representative of order and nurture, Governor Bellingham, and the representative of instinct and nature, Mistress Hibbins, are brother and sister? She strides in the middle world of the Word-made-Flesh as equally an airy sprite as an infant dryad in just being herself, a little girl. Between what we can picture as the extreme circles of the town and the forest which form the manifold geography of the novel (with their real and titular rulers, Governor Bellingham and Mistress Hibbins), a viable center circle emerges as Arthur and Hester (less extreme embodiments of the prevailing disjunction) move toward each other through and in Pearl. It is the matter of Christianity and the instinct of humanity (their spirit was never lost) which the novel recovers in her. She does seem to sit with great numinosity at a sacred center: "So magnificent was the small figure, when thus arrayed, and such was the splendor of Pearl's own proper beauty, shining through the gorgeous robes which might have extinguished a paler loveliness, that there was an absolute circle of radiance around her, on the darksome cottage-floor" (90). This image seems to confirm the rightness of Mr. Wilson's impression which we are surely meant to compare it with. His image of the sun "shining through a richly painted window" reverberates with the echo of Pearl's beauty "shining through gorgeous robes". Indeed she is her own celebrant. Her incarnational aspect is underscored by the

---

[77]   In other works Hawthorne is similarly intrigued with stained glass. In *The Marble Faun* he lingers over it again as emblematic of the Incarnational and Eucharistic base of his moral and artistic view. In Chapter XXXIII we read: "It is the special excellence of pictured glass, that the light, which falls merely on the outside of other pictures, is here interfused throughout the work; it illuminates the design, and invests it with a living radiance; and, in requital, the unfading colours transmute the common daylight into a miracle of richness and glory, in its passage through the heavenly substance of the blessed and angelic shapes, which throng the high-arched window" (IV, 304).

"absolute circle of radiance" – and once again on a floor, the darksome cottage's.[78]

Here then is Hawthorne's chiasm, "A letter, – the letter A" (178), one limb spirit and one limb matter, with Pearl, herself a symbol, the connecting link between those two. No less than Emerson had Hawthorne fulfilled what George Ripley defined in the *Dial* as the transcendentalists' "mission of the present". The same text applies to Hawthorne too: "Spiritualism and materialism both have their foundation in our nature, and both will exist and exert their influence. Shall they exist as antagonist principles?... Here then is the mission of the present. We are to reconcile spirit and matter... Nothing else remains for us to do. Stand still we cannot. To go back is equally impossible."[79] Hawthorne was indeed serious when he said that there was some deep meaning in the letter most worthy of interpretation. That deep meaning can perhaps best be summarized in a definition of art which satisfies Hawthorne's inclusive demands and allusive practice: "Art is the wedding of the masculine intellect... and the feminine power... whose child is a winged word... A true work of art is a Divine Incarnation... a union of the sacred and profane, the eternal and secular."[80]

[78] In terms of the images of light and dark in the passage, compare William Barrett's explanation of the myth of the soul in Plato's *Phaedrus:* "Reason, as the divine part of man, is separated, is indeed of another nature, from the animal within him. We are a long distance here from another symbol of light and dark which early mankind, this time the Chinese, handed down to us: the famous diagram of the forces of *yin* and *yang*, in which the light and the dark lie down beside each other within the same circle, the dark area penetrated by a spot of light and the light by a spot of dark, to symbolize that each must borrow from the other, that the light has need of the dark, and conversely, in order for either to be complete. In Plato's myth first appears that cleavage between reason and the irrational that it has been the long burden of the West to carry, until the dualism makes itself felt in most violent form within modern culture" (*Irrational Man* [Garden City, N.Y., 1962], 83). This long burden of dualism appears in America as Puritanism. Hawthorne builds his novel on dualisms, on the Phaedrus myth, but only to show the opposition of such a viewpoint to the richer comprehension of the antique Christian message – the Pearl myth, which says that "each must borrow from the other, that the light has need of the dark, and conversely, in order for either to be complete".

[79] Quoted in Charles Feidelson, Jr., *Symbolism and American Literature*, 115. Cf. Jolande Jacobi, *The Psychology of C. G. Jung*, trans. Ralph Manheim (New Haven, Conn., 1964), 130-131: "The archetypal image of this *coincidentia oppositorum*, this transformation of the opposites into a third term, a higher synthesis, is expressed by the so-called UNITING SYMBOL which represents the partial systems of the psyche as *united* on a *superordinate*, higher plane. All the symbols and archetypal figures in which the process is embodied are vehicles of the *transcendent function*, that is, of the union of the different pairs of psychic opposites in a synthesis which transcends them both."

[80] Fabian Gudas, "Ananda K. Coomaraswamy: The Perennial Philosophy of Art", *Studies in Comparative Literature*, ed. Waldo F. McNeir (Baton Rouge, 1962), 27.

# PART THREE

IV

# CONTEMPORARY ROMANTICISM

## 1. T. S. ELIOT: THE THIRD BESIDE YOU

> Oh, hours of childhood
> when behind the symbols was more than merely
> the past, and before us was not the future.
>
> Rainer Maria Rilke

T. S. Eliot's poetry is almost uniquely one piece. "The Love Song of J. Alfred Prufrock" leads into *The Waste Land* which is continued and furthered in *Ash-Wednesday* which in turn is finished in the *Four Quartets*. Each poem stands alone and has a life of its own but they are all one life continually building, all one poetry continually evolving with "Christ Jesus Himself the chief cornerstone".[1] Such a cornerstone seems dubious indeed for the love song of Prufrock, but nevertheless the building begins in earnest here. Prufrock errs in undershooting, as Faust had erred in Goethe's drama or the poet in Shelley's *Alastor* by overshooting the synthesis of the self which can be won only by an equal process of finitizing and infinitizing.[2] The characteristic despair of the nineteenth century personified in Faust "who leads a fantastic existence in abstract endeavor after infinity",[3] now gives way in the twentieth to its opposite which rests content with the everyday and the passable, just the *Vergängliche* so intolerant to Faust. One record of this historic and psychological transition from the despair of infinitude to the despair of finitude is Hawthorne's short story "Ethan Brand". Strangely – or not so strangely if one reads Eliot's essay on Baudelaire – Hawthorne dramatizes Ethan's

---

[1] T. S. Eliot, *Collected Poems 1909-1962* (New York, 1963), "Choruses from 'The Rock'", 152. When necessary, page references to this edition are in the text.
[2] See Kierkegaard, *Fear and Trembling* and *The Sickness unto Death*, quoted above, page 47.
[3] Kierkegaard, 165.

sin of Faustian hunger with considerable nostalgia. It seems ennobling, as the submerged imagery of Christ's passion suggests, in comparison and contrast with the new kind of enervating satisfaction which makes its parallel appearance with the growing industry of the little New England town. In days past Ethan had kept the fire burning at the lime-kiln; now Bartram watches it but a deeper fire has died out:

It is a lonesome, and, when the character is inclined to thought, may be an intensely thoughtful occupation; as it proved in the case of Ethan Brand, who had mused to such strange purpose, in days gone by, while the fire in this very kiln was burning.
The man who now watched the fire was of a different order, and troubled himself with no thoughts save the very few that were requisite to his business.[4]

By comparison with the new thoughtlessness the fiend himself is sancti-fied.[5] Characteristically Bartram finds his kiln "half a bushel the richer" for Ethan's bones – bones which the last line of the story calls "relics". When Ethan's bones crumble into relics we leave the nineteenth century and in the person of Bartram we enter the twentieth, the world of J. Alfred Prufrock. Kierkegaard's words delineate the difference between Faust and Prufrock, between the two centuries: "But while one sort of despair plunges wildly into the infinite and loses itself, a second sort permits itself as it were to be defrauded by 'the others'. By seeing the multitude of men about it, by getting engaged in all sorts of worldly affairs, by becoming wise about how things go in this world, such a man forgets himself, forgets what his name is (in the divine understanding of it), does not dare to believe in himself, finds it too venturesome a thing to be himself, far easier and safer to be like the others, to become an imitation, a number, a cipher in the crowd".[6] Against the words of Faust to Mephistopheles,

> If to the moment I should say:
> Abide, you are so fair –
> Put me in fetters on that day,
> I *wish* to perish then, I swear[7]

---

[4]  *Great Short Works of Hawthorne*, ed. Frederick C. Crews (New York, 1967), 352.
[5]  See the essay on Baudelaire in T. S. Eliot, *Selected Essays* (New York, 1950), esp. 378-379: "To a mind observant of the post-Voltaire France... the possibility of damnation is so immense a relief in a world of electoral reform, plebiscites, sex reform and dress reform, that damnation itself is an immediate form of salvation – of salvation from the ennui of modern life, because it at last gives some significance to living."
[6]  Kierkegaard, 166-167.
[7]  Goethe's *Faust*, trans. Walter Kaufmann (Garden City, N.Y., 1963), 185.
      "Werd ich zum Augenblicke sagen:

we now have the easier and safer words of Prufrock who finds it too venturesome to dare disturb the universe:

> No! I am not Prince Hamlet, nor was meant to be;
> Am an attendant lord, one that will do
> To swell a progress, start a scene or two,
> Advise the prince; no doubt, an easy tool,
> Deferential, glad to be of use,
> Politic, cautious, and meticulous...

Life is triply removed: it is a play, and Prufrock acts on the fringe of an imitation. Still, he is in the right play; he knows what is gone.

"This form of despair", Kierkegaard wrote, "is hardly ever noticed in the world."[8] It is hardly noticed because it is paradoxically undignified by the hells in the nineteenth century and earlier that were so vividly ready to receive Fausts and Brands. The only thing waiting to receive Prufrock is the dirty city and the public:

> ... it seems that something has happened that has never happened before:
> though we know not just when, or why, or how, or where.
> Men have left God not for other gods... but for no god...
>
> ("The Rock", 163-164)

> And the wind shall say: "Here were decent godless people:
> Their only monument the asphalt road
> And a thousand lost golf balls."
>
> ("The Rock", 156)

This new despair is then a lack of what Faust possessed, just as his despair was a lack of what Prufrock possesses. The drama of the self's task is still the same and just as delicate, but it is a task which Eliot embraces: to discover the point of intersection and interpenetration, "a white light still and moving" (177) between infinite longing and ineffable rest, the dream and the fact:

> The Lord who created must wish us to create
> And employ our creation again in His service
> Which is already His service in creating.
> For Man is joined spirit and body,
> And therefore must serve as spirit and body.
> Visible and invisible, two worlds meet in Man;
> Visible and invisible must meet in His Temple...
>
> ("The Rock", 168)

---

Verweile doch! Du bist so schön!
Dann magst du mich in Fesseln schlagen,
Dann will ich gern zugrunde gehn!"

[8] Kierkegaard, 167.

Two men in history for Eliot were notably self-possessed. Dante and Pascal are ideal figures for him in this special respect. In Pascal, he writes, we "follow the process of the mind of the intelligent believer" who "finds himself inexorably committed to the dogma of the Incarnation".[9] He becomes inexorably committed because the Incarnation is the model of the self's desired synthesis of infinitude and finitude, a synthesis that Pascal, in Eliot's chiastic description, did achieve: "Pascal is a man of the world among ascetics, and an ascetic among men of the world; he had the knowledge of worldliness and the passion of asceticism, and in him the two are fused into an individual whole."[10] Eliot recommends his work to those who have a similarly unified sensibility, "to those who doubt, but who have the mind to conceive, and the sensibility to feel... and who can only find peace through a satisfaction of the whole being".[11] In his essay on Dante, Eliot proceeds in a similarly dialectical fashion from the mind and the feelings to both in whole being. The discussion of Dante is more literary than religious, but the religious dimension is still powerfully present behind a view of poetic form. Eliot finds Dante "extremely easy to read" and remarks – we can remember Hawthorne puzzling over the scarlet letter – that "genuine poetry can communicate before it is understood".[12] Dante is easy to read because he expresses his ideas in images and these images communicate with something deeper in man than his intellect or reason; they appeal, like the scarlet letter, to the imagination. It is that dormant faculty in modern man that Dante also awakens. And Eliot acutely remarks, "What we should consider is not so much the meaning of the images, but the reverse process, that which led a man having an idea to express it in images."[13] What leads a man to express ideas in images is a world-view in which mystery prevails over problem and where meaning and feeling alike are part and parcel of Being. In other words, Dante imagines in the Coleridgean sense, which Eliot endorses indirectly in praising Dante, and he imagines because he lived in what he saw. Because he sees the eternal through and in the temporal he stylistically gives his literature that symbolic sight: he thinks in images. And while his work reconciles the idea and the image, it also balances them because "in our awareness of the image we must

9    *Selected Essays*, 360.
10   *Selected Essays*, 363.
11   *Selected Essays*, 368.
12   *Selected Essays*, 200.
13   *Selected Essays*, 204.

be aware that the meaning is there too".[14] Dante's art follows quite naturally and vitally from the mutual exchange in which nature is thought and thought nature. Thus in the *Vita Nuova*, Eliot remarks, is "an account of a particular kind of experience: that is, of something which had actual experience... *and* intellectual and imaginative experience... as its materials; and which became a third kind". As a third kind, the *Vita Nuova* "cannot be classed either as 'truth' or 'fiction'".[15] It can be classed, however, as a neutral territory where the actual and the imaginary meet and imbue themselves with the nature of the other. It can be classed as Romantic art. Eliot is on record as a classicist but his approval of Pascal as a man and of Dante as an artist attests to his Romanticism: the life of the one and the literature of the other rest on the Incarnation. As Hugh Fausset wrote, "Jesus' conception of life was ultimately poetic. It represented, like every work of art, a perfect fusion of reason and instinct in imagination."[16] This is the heart of Eliot's work: the diastole of his criticism and the systole of his poetry.

If we do not know just when or why or how or where men left God for no god, Eliot is more definite about a closely related time when reason and instinct fell separately away from the imaginative view: "In the seventeenth century a dissociation of sensibility set in, from which we have never recovered..."[17] Poets continued to think but unlike Dante they did not feel their thought, and their thought was separate from experience. It was against this human, epistemological, and ultimately theological dissociation that Coleridge reasserted the imagination defined as the balance or reconciliation of "the idea, with the image" and of "judgment ever awake and steady self-possession, with enthusiasm and feeling profound or vehement". Emerson referred to "the corruption of man" and Eliot to the dissociation of man, but whatever the emphasis the artist must counter the corruption or dissociation by fastening words again to visible things. Starting with language, by thinking in images man can unify reason and instinct in himself, then himself with the world, and the world he is in again with God. The lines that begin the fifth section of *Ash-Wednesday* suggest how intimate the poet's search for the right word is with the man's search for Christ in Eliot's canon:

If the lost word is lost, if the spent word is spent
If the unheard, unspoken

14  *Loc. cit.*
15  *Selected Essays*, 233.
16  *The Proving of Psyche*, 79.
17  *Selected Essays*, 247.

Word is unspoken, unheard;
Still is the unspoken word, the Word unheard,
The Word without a word, the Word within
The world and for the world;

. . . . . . . . . . . . . . . . . . . . .
Where shall the word be found, where will the word
Resound?

A direct relationship is established throughout Eliot's work between religious debility and imaginative failure. As the Word-made-Flesh fades from modern consciousness so proportionately do

Words strain,
Crack and sometimes break, under the burden,
Under the tension, slip, slide, perish,
Decay with imprecision, will not stay in place,
Will not stay still.

("Burnt Norton", V)

Words "are only hints and guesses, / Hints followed by guesses" because

The hint half guessed, the gift half understood, is Incarnation.
Here the impossible union
Of spheres of existence is actual,
Here the past and future
Are conquered and reconciled...

("The Dry Salvages", V)

The impossible union is of finitude and infinitude, the self's task "which can be performed only by means of a relationship to God".[18] But first God must be found and for Eliot we begin with language by learning to make our words flesh, by fastening ideas to visible things just as, in the verse of Thomas Aquinas, "Verbum caro panem verum / Verbo carnem efficit" (the Word still flesh made the bread flesh by a word).[19] Eliot would learn to say the word so that we see the Word. Poetry then becomes prayer, and an inability to pray is an inability to reconcile and balance the idea and the image in imaginatively prayerful imitation of Christ. In this way, as Walter Ong remarks of medieval literature, "the very texture of poetry itself – the element which makes literature litera-

---

[18]   Kierkegaard, 162.
[19]   Quoted by Walter Ong, "Wit and Mystery: A Revaluation in Mediaeval Latin Hymnody", *Speculum*, XXII (1947), 316. The verse is from the vesper hymn *Pange Lingua* in the Roman breviary under the office of Corpus Christi. Cf. the lines from "Sweeney Among the Nightingales": "The host [the Eucharist] with someone indistinct [the priest] / Converses [makes poetry with] at the door apart" (the opened tabernacle).

ture – is seen to come into functional contact with the heart of Christian doctrine, the mysteries distinctive of Christianity as these lie in their own distinctive way within the human mind".[20]

With Eliot too, then, we should first consider not so much the meaning of his images, of the garden and the desert and the withered apple-seed for example, but rather what led him having ideas about the Fall of Man, "Adam's curse" (188) and "the primitive terror" (195), to express them in images. One reason is that such expression runs counter to the current of the Fall that is so frequently the subject. Poetically, redemption lies in the garden of linguistics. However much we choose to quibble with Eliot's notion of the objective correlative, it fits in with his admiration for Pascal and Dante and with his description of the dissociation of sensibility: "The only way of expressing emotion in the form of art is by finding an 'objective correlative'; in other words, a set of objects, a situation, a chain of events which shall be the formula of that *particular* emotion; such that when the external facts, which must terminate in sensory experience, are given, the emotion is immediately evoked."[21] The emphasis in all his remarks is on closing gaps – between worldliness and asceticism, thought and emotion, the idea and the image, and between expression and experience:

> And the end of all our exploring
> Will be to arrive where we started
> And know the place for the first time.
> Through the unknown, remembered gate
> When the last of earth left to discover
> Is that which was the beginning;
> At the source of the longest river
> The voice of the hidden waterfall
> And the children in the apple-tree...
>
> ("Little Gidding", V)

The voyage is round the world across the desert of dualism to the back gate of the garden of Being, Paradise, from which man had first driven himself in coming to know that he lived in what he saw:

> Go, said the bird, for the leaves were full of children,
> Hidden excitedly, containing laughter.
> Go, go, go, said the bird: human kind
> Cannot bear very much reality.
> Time past and time future

[20] "Wit and Mystery...", 312.
[21] *Selected Essays*, 124-125.

What might have been and what has been
Point to one end, which is always present.[22]

("Burnt Norton", I)

Between the loss and the recovery the poet steers his way in paradox
through "the waste sad time / Stretching before and after" (181) the loss of
time itself in the fall from the eternally present moment of Being:

Words, after speech, reach
Into the silence. Only by the form, the pattern,
Can words or music reach
The stillness, as a Chinese jar still
Moves perpetually in its stillness.
Not the stillness of the violin, while the note lasts,
Not that only, but the co-existence...

("Burnt Norton", V)

Through such a form and pattern the poet gathers the past and the future
together in the one moment paradox uncovers – the symbolic moment
of Incarnation "transecting, bisecting the world of time, a moment in
time but not like a moment of time" (163). This is the moment of redemption, the at-one-ment beyond the past and the future because
"Between the blossom- and the fruit-time" (138) as "a third kind".

Time past and time future point as right and left angles to the third still
point which is always present:

At the still point of the turning world. Neither flesh nor fleshless;
Neither from nor towards; at the still point, there the dance is,
But neither arrest nor movement. And do not call it fixity,
Where past and future are gathered.[23]

("Burnt Norton", II)

[22]   See Robert Wagner, "The Meaning of Eliot's Rose Garden", *PMLA*, LXIX (1954),
26: "The significant quality of the original experience (revived in the rose-garden)
was its unself-consciousness. We were then innocently at one with reality. But alien
influences distracted us from the meaning; we could not 'bear very much reality,'
and were expelled from the garden ('Go, go, go, said the bird'). And now, except for
rare, 'unattended' moments, we are no longer, and in our human state can never be,
at one with reality. Though we have, through memory, approached the meaning of
our experience – and that is a beginning – we cannot rest happily in the experience
itself because we have recovered it in 'a different form.' We have recovered it only in
the form of an image, an echo, and in our daily lives we feel ourselves separated by a
terrible dualism from the permanent reality represented by that image or heard in
that echo.
   It is therefore the lot of human consciousness to be unable to approach reality
directly; it can do so only through the medium of the imagination."
[23]   See Lawrence Durrell, "The Other T. S. Eliot", *Atlantic*, CCXV (1965), 60:
"When I grew to know him a little better and to value his own creative richness at its

Thus when Eliot writes in *Tradition and the Individual Talent* of the need to cultivate in writing an "historical sense", "which is a sense of the timeless as well as of the temporal and of the timeless and of the temporal together",[24] we can see now how this too is based on a more encompassing theological sense with inclusive literary ramifications. A rich example of the practice of this double and single sense by Eliot is the following passage from the third section of *Ash-Wednesday:*

> At the first turning of the third stair
> Was a slotted window bellied like the fig's fruit
> And beyond the hawthorn blossom and a pasture scene
> The broadbacked figure drest in blue and green
> Enchanted the maytime with an antique flute.
> Blown hair is sweet, brown hair over the mouth blown,
> Lilac and brown hair;
> Distraction, music of the flute, stops and steps of the mind over the third
> stair,
> Fading, fading; strength beyond hope and despair
> Climbing the third stair.
>
> Lord, I am not worthy
> Lord, I am not worthy
>
> but speak the word only

The poet seems to be overcoming the last temptations of earth's pleasures, for earth offers him another rebirth through the "slotted window bellied" into a pastoral land of natural joy and peace. The labor is a lingering, then, as well it should be in a glimpse of such natural grace. And for another reason too: the enchanting vision is not the distraction it is called for it is being divinized and supernaturalized ironically at the same time the poet is pulling away. As he moves away from the temporal towards the timeless, the timeless in reverse is moving into the temporal even through the window bellied like the fig's fruit (Mary's womb and the Tabernacle),[25] for the words "Lord, I am not worthy" are said in

---

true worth I took the liberty of arranging the letters of his name thus, Tse-Lio-T, to suggest that there was a Chinese Taoist sage lurking under the sober cloak of his Anglo-Catholicism; the change amused him, and he did not demur. I think he probably felt that dogmatic theology aside, there was a suitable kind of root experience between the rarest and ripest experience in both ways of viewing the world – the Eastern and the Western." Cf. Walden as "God's Drop".

[24]  *Selected Essays*, 4.
[25]  Cf. the description of Mary in "The Dry Salvages" IV as "Figlia del tuo figlio" (daughter of thy son).

the Mass just before reception of the Eucharist – distributed, through association, by the broadbacked figure in blue and green, i.e. the shepherd as priest in chasuble the colors of heaven and earth.[26] Man, then, going to God meets God in coming to man. The chiastic moment on the "third stair" of Communion establishes the difference between the temporal and the timeless but also a sense of the temporal and the timeless together.[27] "He who is the Lord of all things", as William Lynch wrote, "is the lord of the imagination."[28] He is the lord, in any case, of this Romantic imagination, Eliot's, which reveals itself in such balance and in such reconciliation.

Through the direct and indirect references to the Incarnation it is clear that Eliot's central theme is the spiritualization of matter and the materialization of spirit through symbolization. Like Coleridge and Wordsworth together, he desires in his own work to supernaturalize the natural and to naturalize the supernatural because the central moment of history for him is the birth of Christ, "The point of intersection of the timeless / With time" (198). Surely the beginning of his career was as revolutionary as theirs. What they had stated and done had to be stated and done again. Poetry had become reflective: poets "thought and felt by fits, unbalanced..."[29]. Eliot traced this lack of balance and failure of imagination, as Elizabeth Drew has written, "to the specific loss of direct symbolic transformation as a method of perception".[30] People lived and people saw, but they no longer lived in what they saw the way Dante and Pascal had: a living and a seeing at once that had determined their symbolic perception. This sense of whole being is what Eliot battled to recapture and revitalize for modern man in his own verse. In the words of Elizabeth Drew, "Eliot wanted to recapture all the concentration which the symbol

[26] As Theodore Spencer has noted, the background of *Ash-Wednesday* "is not a pagan ritual, but the Catholic Mass. The waste land has been crossed, and on the other side is the Christian religion." "The Poetry of T. S. Eliot", *Atlantic*, CLI (1933), 66. The words at Mass, said three times before Communion, were: "Lord, I am not worthy that You should come under my roof; but only say the word, and my soul will be healed."

[27] Cf. Theodore Morrison, "*Ash-Wednesday*: A Religious History", *NEQ*, XI (1938), 281: "It could almost be said that the very theme of *Ash-Wednesday* lies in this close relation between natural interest in the immediate world, of which the best evidence is fruitfulness of some kind, productivity of mind or body, and the possibility of believing in the divine, in a world transcending the natural. The two are bound together by an inscrutable linkage at the source of human nature." The same linkage is what so intrigued Eliot in the Grail legend.

[28] *Christ and Apollo*, 158.

[29] *Selected Essays*, 248.

[30] *T. S. Eliot: The Design of His Poetry* (New York, 1949), 17.

brings as a result of the kind of perception in which object and 'meaning' synchronize and are recognized simultaneously. And not a single 'meaning,' since no symbol can ever be pinned down to that. As it embodies both thought and sensation, so all the potential proliferation of physical life itself, and all the *relating* qualities of thinking, live in it together. It is body and mind in one: it both means and is."[31] Symbolic perception is the same as mythic perception and the relation between mythic language and religion – and the loss of both – has been clarified by Ernst Cassirer in words which suggest why Eliot, like Coleridge, turned to mythic or symbolic writing as the inevitable ramification of his essentially religious critique of life and literature. In myth, wrote Cassirer, there is a "hypostatization or transubstantiation" of language where "the word... is merged with its object in an indissoluble unity"; "in place of a more or less adequate 'expression,' we find a relation of identity, of complete congruence between 'image' and 'object,' between the name and the thing".[32] What is said, then, is seen. There is no abstraction or drawing away of words from things to roam freely and imprecisely among different things because man has not abstracted himself from his environment and therefore does not think or feel by fits, unbalanced. Myth posits a balance in man between thought and feeling based on a further and deeper balance between man and nature in Being, and for Eliot of the human and divine natures in Christ. From this context we can perhaps better understand what Eliot wrote in "Little Gidding" (II) of the renewed literary revolution: "our concern was speech, and speech impelled us / To purify the dialect of the tribe". Like Hawthorne, Eliot searched in the past for the living hieroglyph. The inheritance is a rich one to be distributed through his verse:

> We have taken from the defeated
> What they had to leave us – a symbol:
> A symbol perfected in death.
> And all shall be well and
> All manner of thing shall be well
> By the purification of the motive
> In the ground of our beseeching.

("Little Gidding", III)

The waste land is waste to begin with because of a lack of this mythic or symbolic perception in the protagonist. It is doubly ironical that many

[31] *T. S. Eliot: The Design of His Poetry*, 18.
[32] *Language and Myth*, 58.

readers look for explanations of *The Waste Land* before the poem has had a chance to communicate the fundamental questions it raises through its symbolic form about the nature of explanation itself. In this way it is indeed related to *The Rime of the Ancient Mariner* as a modern version of that ballad. What is told is intimate with the way of telling to the point that we see that the speaker, like the ancient mariner, already has the experience of the waste land behind him. He no longer thinks or feels by fits, unbalanced, because this very loss of wholeness is told to the reader, the protagonist's wedding guest, in a mythic language that is a testimony to his having achieved the goal of the initiation and journey he relates – the winning of the self beyond the true self that only thinks and the false self that only feels. This time in place of the shooting of the albatross, which Coleridge used as his objective correlative, the catalyst of the journey is an experience in the hyacinth garden:

> – Yet when we came back, late, from the hyacinth garden,
> Your arms full, and your hair wet, I could not
> Speak, and my eyes failed, I was neither
> Living nor dead, and I knew nothing
> Looking into the heart of light, the silence.

("The Burial of the Dead")

The rest of the poem alternates between images which refer to a lost and golden time and images which refer to various sordid sexual encounters. This sustained contrast suggests that the experience in the garden was a sexual one preceded by innocent infatuation and followed by an equal disgust. The one flushed moment in the garden hovers ambiguously between the two attitudes, for expectation has not yet dwindled through fulfillment; the future has not quite become the past. It does soon enough, however. The line *"Oed' und leer das Meer"* (Desolate and empty the sea) follows upon "Looking into the heart of light, the silence" and indicates a profound feeling of loss and let-down. The line is from Wagner's opera *Tristan und Isolde,* and it means that Isolde's ship is nowhere in sight. But in the poem this sense is exactly reversed by the context of love satisfied in the garden, while the original sense of the reference itself, love unsatisfied, is still heard to intensify and define the anguished contrast of before and after which the speaker feels. The experience of sex has not lived up to the infinite promise of infatuation intimated in other lines from Wagner which immediately precede the moment in the garden:

*Frisch weht der Wind*
*Der Heimat zu*
*Mein Irisch Kind*
*Wo weilest du?*[33]

With *"Oed' und leer das Meer"* love's imaginary food becomes the "greasy relics" of Troilus' similar lament. "Twit twit twit" has become "jug jug jug / So rudely forc'd" (61). The whole passage from dream to fact to disillusion was forecast in the concluding lines of "The Love Song of J. Alfred Prufrock":

> We have lingered in the chambers of the sea
> By sea-girls wreathed with seaweed red and brown
> Till human voices wake us, and we drown.

This is the root experience which sends the speaker through the waste land or soulscape of his own disgust in order to make the arid garden of love bloom again in such a way that past and future will be contained in a present which enfolds and gathers expectation and fulfillment alike. This is the garden to come later in *Ash-Wednesday* which must be read, with the *Four Quartets*, in conjunction with *The Waste Land:*

> The single Rose
> Is now the Garden
> Where all loves end
> Terminate torment
> Of love unsatisfied
> The greater torment
> Of love satisfied... (II)

In the hyacinth garden, however, the two loves are mutually exclusive. Unlike Prufrock, the protagonist has more than popped the question; and *The Waste Land* is the magic lantern which throws his "nerves in patterns on a screen" for his uneasy viewing and ours. Prufrock was apparently right about commitment after all, for the protagonist sees himself as a small noxious thing "pinned and wriggling on the wall". The torment of love unsatisfied has led to the greater torment of love satisfied and this love ramifies into objective correlatives of guilt and disgust throughout the poem: the scene in the first part of "A Game of Chess" which apparently evokes an image of Cleopatra waiting for Antony but which now on the same terms – after sex – suggests an expensive brothel jammed with bric-a-brac, golden Cupids and carved dolphins, where a lady drowned in cheap perfume sits by the window;

---

[33] "The wind blows fresh / to the homeland: / my Irish child, / where are you lingering?"

the casual allusions in the second part to marital life which has become
a matter of getting false teeth and abortions; and particularly the scenes
throughout "The Fire Sermon" which follow the speaker's reiteration
of what it was that makes him see all the things he does see – "The
nymphs are departed"; the ideal and Impossible She of his infatuated
mind has turned into the prostitute of his conscience after fulfillment in
the garden: there is the rat dragging its slimy belly through the vegetation;
white bodies naked on the ground; there is Sweeney who will come to
Mrs. Porter instead of – before the garden – Actaeon to Diana; Mr.
Eugenides, the homosexual, who offers luncheon and a weekend at the
Metropole; the carbuncular young man whose "Exploring hands encounter no defence" and whose "vanity requires no response, / And
makes a welcome of indifference"; and above all the three Thames-
daughters who indifferently sing of their violation: "By Richmond I
raised my knees / Supine on the floor of a narrow canoe"; "I made no
comment. What should I resent?"; "I can connect / Nothing with
nothing." All these scenes follow from the line "*Oed' und leer das Meer*".
They are all objective correlatives for the sexual nausea which the speaker
feels within himself for having lost his innocence and with woman for
having betrayed his idealization of her, for having become a Thames-
daughter of the polluted river of the adult present instead of remaining a
Rhine-maiden in the clean water of the childlike past. Conscience here is
indeed ecologically minded.

The waste land is waste, therefore, because the protagonist sees what
he feels – as an anxious and lonely Robin sees crooked streets and empty
churches in Hawthorne's "My Kinsman, Major Molineux". In his poem
Eliot is no more condemning modern society than Hawthorne in his
short story was criticizing city-planning or religious indifference.[34] The
technique is like that of a painting by Chagall: red roosters crow on the
Eiffel Tower and floating purple cows play violins not because 'tis all
in pieces and coherence gone but because love, we say, is like that; it
affects our vision of the world. And a lack of love or a sense of love gone
awry does the same:

[34]  Cf. Eliot's words on Pascal, *Selected Essays*, 364: "Pascal's disillusioned analysis
of human bondage is sometimes interpreted to mean that Pascal was really and finally
an unbeliever, who, in his despair, was incapable of enduring reality and enjoying the
heroic satisfaction of the free man's worship of nothing. His despair, his disillusion,
are, however, no illustration of personal weakness; they are perfectly objective, because
they are essential moments in the progress of the intellectual soul; and for the type of
Pascal they are the analogue of the drought, the dark night, which is an essential stage
in the progress of the Christian mystic."

A woman drew her long black hair out tight
And fiddled whisper music on those strings
And bats with baby faces in the violet light
Whistled, and beat their wings
And crawled head downward down a blackened wall...

("What the Thunder Said")

The protagonist of *The Waste Land* magnifies and distorts the world according to the temperature of his own personal moral fever as well as from a physical fright that the hyacinth girl might have conceived and will give birth to his child – contorted through his fear and anguish into a bat with a baby face crawling down a blackened wall. Everywhere he sees what he did – enlarged. He is the barbarous king who has raped and changed Philomel; Sweeney who comes to Mrs. Porter; the clerk who comes to the typist. If he remembers lines from Shakespeare's *The Tempest* and Spenser's *Prothalamion,* he recalls them because the innocent love of Ferdinand and Miranda and nuptial grace stand in such contrast with his own action and in painful memory of what love had been: *"Frisch weht der Wind"*. The primary purpose of such references, and others to Webster, Middleton, Marvell, and Day is not to underscore the rampant lust or sexual indifference of the modern world but to show the high temperature of the protagonist's own guilt: he has made the world modern in himself. "London Bridge is falling down falling down falling down": it isn't, though; but what has fallen down in the speaker is childhood with all its nursery rhymes and innocence. He remembers it by fits and starts which only compound the sense of dereliction: *"Et O ces voix d'enfants, chantant dans la coupole"* (III, 202).

The line about childrens' voices from the choir is from Verlaine's *Parsifal,* and has the double function of looking two ways: it shows the speaker's nostalgia for his lost childlikeness, a purity associated with worship, and it points the way forward to the Chapel Perilous where he must go, like Parsifal in quest of the Grail, if he is to find the interconnection between temporal love and timeless love deep within himself but mythologized externally as the Grail legend he remembers. The goal is not opposite the hyacinth garden where the journey begins, as from the womb of Paradise, but apposite it as the Chapel across the waste land and later as the cloistered garden in *Ash-Wednesday* and as the rose garden in the *Four Quartets* where the "unread vision" or unknown meaning of the hyacinth garden is redeemed "in the higher dream" (90) where "the fire and the rose are one" (209) – where, in Yeats's version, "body is not bruised to pleasure soul".[35] Again, supporting this journey at all times, but especially in *Ash-Wednesday* and the *Four Quartets*, is the poet's own continual search for the right word, for what Eliot called in his essay on Dante "the real right thing"[36] where feeling and thought would so perfectly imbue themselves with the nature of each other that the word would be not only a statement of, but simultaneously a witness to, the higher dream – earth repeated in a finer tone: "Not the stillness of the violin, while the note lasts, / Not that only, but the co-existence" (180).

The insistence on co-existence and the reference to *Parsifal* remind us of Eliot's remark in the preface to his notes on *The Waste Land* that the title and the plan of the poem were suggested to him, along with "a good deal of the incidental symbolism", by Jessie Weston's book on the Grail legend, *From Ritual to Romance*. The general plan, personalized by Eliot, is summarized by Maud Bodkin:

It is the initiation, or rebirth, pattern present in Eliot's poem that seems to me to mould and dominate the emotional response to the whole, when the various internal links and associations have worked their effect upon the mind. After the haunted perilous wanderings, the agony of drought and night and delirium, after we have experienced with almost physical relief the cock's dawn cry and the "damp gust bringing rain," we await the poem's closing message even as a candidate for initiation, after laborious wanderings without issue, journeyings through the dark, full of misgivings and terror and anguish, might await the final redeeming vision.[37]

Jessie Weston not only suggested this plan for the poem, however; she also suggested the content of the redeeming vision of co-existence which became the foundation of Eliot's own poetics and the goal of the protagonist in *The Waste Land*. Two worlds meet in man, as Eliot wrote, spirit and body, and it was this meeting which Eliot found mythologized on a different level in the Grail legend elucidated by Jessie Weston. "If there be a mystery of the Grail", she wrote, "surely the mystery lies here, in the possibility of identifying two objects which, apparently, lie at the very opposite poles of intellectual conception"[38] – the Vessel of natural Plenty and the Eucharistic Chalice of supernatural life: the profane and the sacred. In one passage from her book we can almost see the seed for

---

[35]   From the last stanza of "Among School Children", *The Collected Poems of W. B. Yeats* (New York, 1956), 214.
[36]   *Selected Essays*, 228.
[37]   *Archetypal Patterns in Poetry* (New York, 1958), 303-304.
[38]   *From Ritual to Romance* (Garden City, N.Y., 1957), 139.

Eliot's later expressed admiration of Pascal, who fused "the knowledge of worldliness and the passion of asceticism", and for Donne, who felt his thought, and for Dante, who expressed his ideas in images – as well as the basis for his judgment of men and authors whose sensibilities and styles are less unified and whole: "Yet the men who wrote these romances saw no incongruity in identifying the mysterious Food-providing Vessel of the *Bleheris-Gawain* version with the Chalice of the Eucharist, and in ascribing the power of bestowing Spiritual Life to that which certain modern scholars have identified as a *Wunsch-Ding*, a Folk-tale Vessel of Plenty."[39] She maintains that this identification was possible because of the esoteric side of the Nature Cults where "the worshippers partook of the Food and Drink of Eternal life..."[40] But we should see that it is not the growth of the spiritual out of the biological that caught Eliot's interest; it was rather the close relationship of the two, the very fact that they could even have been brought together, let alone how. The togetherness of the temporal and the eternal initiation captured the imagination of the poet who went on later to lament variously related dissociations from such an inclusive view:

The Exoteric side of the cult gives us the Human, the Folk-lore, elements – the Suffering King; the Waste Land; the effect upon the Folk; the task that lies before the hero; the group of Grail symbols. The Esoteric side provides us with the Mystic Meal, the Food of Life, connected in some mysterious way with a Vessel which is the centre of the cult; the combination of that vessel with a Weapon, a combination bearing a well-known "generative" significance; a double initiation into the source of the lower and higher spheres of Life; the ultimate proof of the successful issue of the final test in the restoration of the King.[41]

For the protagonist of *The Waste Land*, though, such an identity of the Vessel and the Chalice where the body's and soul's needs are met at once is entirely incongruous. For him, to use Keats, there is no mediation between the two initiations, love's ripening breast and the steadfastness of the bright star. The lower and higher human loyalties cancel each other out. Like Keats's knight-at-arms alone and palely loitering, the protagonist in Eliot's garden-version of the elfin-grot awakes, if not on a cold

---

[39] *Loc. cit.* Cf. *Selected Essays*, 247: "the ordinary man's experience is chaotic, irregular, fragmentary. The latter falls in love, or reads Spinoza, and these two experiences have nothing to do with each other, or with the noise of the typewriter or the smell of cooking; in the mind of the poet these experiences are always forming new wholes."
[40] *From Ritual to Romance*, 168.
[41] *From Ritual to Romance*, 158-159.

hill-side, in the desert of sexual horror and self-loathing: "The sedge has withered from the Lake": *"Oed' und leer das Meer"*:

To Carthage then I came

Burning burning burning burning
O Lord Thou pluckest me out
O Lord Thou pluckest

burning

("The Fire Sermon")

Just after the experience in the garden he seeks out the fortune-teller Madame Sosostris. She knows what ails the typical young man well enough to give him the right cards. The hyacinth girl is La Belle Dame sans Merci, the card in the Tarot pack of "Belladonna, the Lady of the Rocks, / The lady of situations". His own card, tellingly, is the drowned Phoenician Sailor. And Madame Sosostris suggests to him in an aside – in her job she has to be positive – that there is light at the end of the tunnel. She significantly quotes from *The Tempest*, the idyl of young love, and says "(Those are pearls that were his eyes. Look!)". Something beautiful will come out of his difficulty but it will be won only through pain and a kind of baptismal death that will lead to a new way of seeing what now only shocks him. Another card, flipped quickly, is "the man with three staves". In his note on the Tarot pack, Eliot says that he "quite arbitrarily" associated this card with the Fisher King. Such arbitrariness in any case is "the real right thing", for exactly as the man with three staves the Fisher King makes explicit a "third kind" of meaning from the two opposite meanings implicit in the symbol of the fish: from water, the life of the body through food, and through purification and baptism the life of the spirit. He is therefore "the essential centre of the whole cult" of the Grail drama and of the psychodrama in *The Waste Land:* he is "a being semi-divine, semi-human" whose title expresses "the intention and object of the perplexing whole..."[42] The object is the satisfaction of the whole being. The affinity of the Fisher King with Christ is clear if only in the fact that in early Christianity the Greek word for fish, ICH-THUS, became the acrostic of "Jesus Christ, Son of God, Saviour".[43]

---

[42]  *From Ritual to Romance*, 136.
[43]  See Jean Daniélou, *Primitive Christian Symbols*, trans. Donald Attwater (Baltimore, 1964), 50. The fish generally appears in a baptismal context in the writings of the Latin Fathers and in the paintings in the catacombs. The fourth section of *The Waste Land*, "Death by Water", has this baptismal meaning (see St. Paul, *Romans* 6:3: "when we were baptised in Christ Jesus we were baptised in his death") which is

But behind the acrostic itself is the symbol which is a witness to what the acrostic states: in Christ the natural and the supernatural conjoin; he is fully human and fully divine. At the moment, though, the protagonist can not perceive this dynamic gathering; the Fisher King is impotent to him and the third realm he rules is arid. Nevertheless the person of the Fisher King points the way to "a third kind" of personality which the young man must awaken beyond what he considers his true and sacred self in the long lost past and the false and profane self of the present. He can only find peace by dying to either self alone in order to find "a satisfaction of the whole being". When he has done this he will come to another group of rocks, this time the Dry Salvages in the *Four Quartets*, and see that Belladonna, in the higher and redeeming dream, is the Lady "whose shrine stands on the promontory" and who is invoked as the protectress of those, like himself, "Whose business has to do with fish" (197). What had been rejected as poisonous will come to be hailed as full of grace. The requirements of the journey for the recovery of the garden are clear:

> Whisper of running streams, and winter lightning.
> The wild thyme unseen and the wild strawberry,
> The laughter in the garden, echoed ecstasy
> Not lost, but requiring, pointing to the agony
> Of death and birth.

> ("East Coker", III)

The agony of death and birth begins almost subliminally through references to the myths of Attis, Adonis, and Osiris from Frazer's *The Golden Bough*. These were deities in primitive fertility cults whose life and death and resurrection coincided with the cycle of the seasons. But perhaps more important than the initiatory pattern of death and regeneration which they enact is the fact that their sacredness was intimately connected and even identified with what they meant on a human plane: they were deities but they were deities of vegetation; their resurrection in the spring made the seeds sprout and the crops grow. In other words, in Attis, Adonis, and Osiris the timeless and the temporal have not yet drawn apart to become asceticism on one side of man's consciousness and worldliness on the other. Their spirit is the body, and the body is their spirit.

---

reinforced by the phrase "Gentile or Jew" through St. Paul's description of all men as one through baptism in Christ (*Galatians* 3:28). See Jessie Weston, 133, for a discussion of the Friday fish-meal which, like the Grail legend, symbolically bridges the sensual and the spiritual.

It is this mythic sense of the proximity of the two which the protagonist needs to recover. (The corollary theme of the imagination is never far behind by implication: men must learn again to feel their thought and, having done so, to express their ideas in images as testimony to the whole being.) The protagonist's first strong remembrance of the myth is almost neurotically related to his own sexual act in the hyacinth garden. He is addressing Stetson but he is talking to himself about himself:

> "That corpse you planted last year in your garden,
> Has it begun to sprout? Will it bloom this year?"
>
>                 ("The Burial of the Dead")

Startling as the reference is, it begins movement that will eventually culminate in affirmation. Like the reference from *Parsifal*, it hovers between two senses that for the moment seem merely to collide and clash – a reference to insemination and a reference to the buried god – but which slowly fuse as the protagonist lessens the distance between the two, between the Vessel and the Chalice, by wandering like the ancient mariner and finding, even through such initially jarring references, that the spirit is an incarnate individual and that his own individuality – hyperbolized in the synecdoche of sex – is therefore reconciled with that in-temporized spirit. The submerged references to the buried gods therefore function as "priestly task" and "snow" in Keats's "Bright Star" sonnet to mediate what Eliot called the "unknown, dark *psychic material* – we might say, the octopus or angel with which the poet struggles".[44] The mediation elevates the merely sexual into love by lowering the solely divine into the human.

In the final section of *The Waste Land*, "What the Thunder Said", the mediation deepens as the protagonist identifies his journey with Christ's agony and death. The imagery of the hyacinth garden is present but submerged and in the process of transformation:

> After the torchlight red on sweaty faces
> After the frosty silence in the gardens
> After the agony in stony places
> The shouting and the crying
> Prison and palace and reverberation
> Of thunder of spring over distant mountains
> He who was living is now dead
> We who were living are now dying
> With a little patience

[44] *On Poetry and Poets* (New York, 1957), 110.

As he wanders like the Jews across the desert of his own personalized
Old Testament, the protagonist by analogy is dying also to the negative
sense of what he feels:

> Here is no water but only rock
> Rock and no water and the sandy road
> The road winding above among the mountains[45]

Finally he does come to the goal of his journey which seems to have been
only a mirage all along:

> In this decayed hole among the mountains
> In the faint moonlight, the grass is singing
> Over the tumbled graves, about the chapel
> There is the empty chapel, only the wind's home.
> It has no windows, and the door swings,
> Dry bones can harm no one.

Still, there is faint moonlight and the grass is singing. This is the time
between – early dawn. The protagonist finds the chapel empty and the
door open – but not because there is no god or hope for regeneration or
that the sense of the chapel's emptiness is a final temptation to be overcome, but because he has already passed Christ on the way: he has risen:

> Who is the third who walks always beside you?
> When I count, there are only you and I together
> But when I look ahead up the white road
> There is always another one walking beside you
> Gliding wrapt in a brown mantle, hooded
> I do not know whether a man or a woman...[46]

This explains why the grass is singing over the tumbled graves huddled
around the chapel-tomb of Christ. And therefore, too, at the empty
chapel there is "a flash of lightning" and "a damp gust / Bringing rain"
to the waste land. Aroused himself beyond the You and I of Prufrock's
angel and octopus, the protagonist can now see ahead to the third, the
point of intersection neither flesh nor fleshless. He is able at last to
return to his early experience so long and strongly rejected, just as the

---

[45] See Daniélou, 56: "A third theme [of living water] is the rock in the wilderness.
Its baptismal interpretation goes back to 1 Cor. 10. 4, which calls Christ the rock from
which living water flows, and to John 7. 38-9."
[46] According to Eliot's introduction, the lines refer to the journey to Emmaus (Luke
24: 13-35). Concerning the last line, "I do not know whether a man or a woman",
see St. Paul, *Galatians* 3:28: "All baptised in Christ, you have all clothed yourselves
in Christ, and there are no more distinctions between Jew and Greek, slave and free,
male and female, but all of you are one in Christ Jesus."

ancient mariner, in his sea-death, had turned through the mediation of the moon to what had been the slimy snakes of his own guilt to bless them as creation's rich attire. The thunder says what the protagonist has come to realize about creation and creaturehood through his long voyage:

> Da
> *Datta:* what have we given?
> My friend, blood shaking my heart
> The awful daring of a moment's surrender
> Which an age of prudence can never retract
> By this, and this only, we have existed

But this affirmed moment of love satisfied is now also identical with the moment of love unsatisfied. As the thunder continues to roll its revelation, it reverberates with the earlier lines from Wagner about innocent and chaste infatuation which had preceded fulfillment in the hyacinth garden. "*Frisch weht der Wind*" now reappears inclusive with the "awful daring of a moment's surrender":

> Da
> *Damyata:* The boat responded
> Gaily, to the hand expert with sail and oar
> The sea was calm, your heart would have responded
> Gaily, when invited, beating obedient
> To controlling hands

Infatuation, "what might have been", no longer leads through sex, "what has been", to an empty and desolate sea. Love has bloomed ahead of them, "Torn and most whole" (87) and "always present". The Incarnation is no longer half-guessed, half-understood for the drowned Phoenician Sailor has become one with the man with three staves, the Fisher King, Christ: "I sat upon the shore / Fishing, with the arid plain behind me."[47] The two torments of love unsatisfied and love satisfied terminate in the impossible union "Between the blossom- and the fruit-time", shed their differences, and create the peace of the imagination which surpasses understanding: "Shantih shantih shantih."

---

[47] See Daniélou, 51.

## 2. SNYDER, STAFFORD, WILBUR, AND NEMEROV: THE SEARCH FOR THE CONCRETE

Praise the world to the angel, not the unutterable world;
you cannot astonish him with your glorious feelings;
in the universe, where he feels more sensitively,
you're just a beginner. Therefore, show him the simple
thing that is shaped in passing from father to son,
that lives near our hands and eyes as our very own.
Tell him about the Things. He'll stand more amazed,
as you stood beside the rope-maker in Rome, or the
potter on the Nile...

Rainer Maria Rilke

The relative scarcity of critical estimations of contemporary American poetry stems from the problems that confront current critical approaches to the new poetry rather than from any want of admiration for it. More is involved than simply gaining distance in time. Often it will not explicate, and for good reasons, reasons in fact that take reason or intellectual judgments to task. This is not always so, as the following pages will make clear; but it happens enough to warrant the tentative generalization that the eye focusing on event has come to replace the mind building in metaphor. However, articles here and there and a few books, notably by Richard Howard and Ralph Mills, Jr., do begin to suggest an over-all picture of this new and highly subjective mode that somehow constitutes a general and objective "poetry of experience", as Donald Hall cogently remarked in his introduction to the excellent Penguin anthology of contemporary American poetry. Poets like Theodore Roethke, John Logan, and James Wright do not retreat behind any mask. There is a disarming honesty about their poetry that has much to do with the tone of compassion and helplessness that seems dominant in so much work today. The new poems are indeed "a riprap on the slick rock of metaphysics".[48] If evil is the systematic substitution of the abstract for the concrete, as Sartre insisted, poetry now substitutes the concrete for the abstract. Instead of reason, "that dreary shed, that hutch for grubby schoolboys", the contemporary poets agree with Theodore Roethke that "the hedgewren's song says something else".[49] Tired of a monstrous knowledge which eats up the world and then feeds on itself, James Wright

---

[48]  Gary Snyder, *Myths & Texts* (New York, 1960), 43.
[49]  From "I Cry, Love! Love!", *The Collected Poems* (Garden City, N.Y., 1966), 92.

simply remarks: "There are good things in this world."[50] He and others
stand in openness to receive them:

> Relieved, I let the book fall behind a stone.
> . . . . . . . . . . . . . . . . . . .
> I close my eyes for a moment, and listen.
> The old grasshoppers
> Are tired, they leap heavily now,
> Their thighs are burdened.
> I want to hear them, they have clear sounds to make.
> Then lovely, far off, a dark cricket begins
> In the maple trees.[51]

Epigraphs for the new mood might be these lines from four of the
contemporary poets –

> from Gary Snyder:    Again the ancient, meaningless
> Abstractions of the educated mind.
>     wet feet and the campfire out.[52]

> Richard Wilbur:    If you cannot cure us without destroying our swine,
> We had rather you shoved off.[53]

> Denise Levertov:    The world is
> Not with us enough.[54]

and William Stafford: It's a light thing, a bounce, to live here.[55]

The voice is different, the mood has changed from the elegant anguish of
Eliot and the ethical importunity of Pound to the silent being-in of Keats's
ode "To Autumn". Like Huckleberry Finn in letting go, the new poets
let the world in. But these lines, while they chart new directions or no
directions at all, make clear at the same time a line of indebtedness to
Pound and Eliot and particularly to William Carlos Williams. These
three are the Furies of the Concrete. Pound inveighs against abstraction;
Eliot offers in its place the love of man and woman as that images man's
relationship with God. What the concrete was for Pound the feminine
became for Eliot: a recovery of something long lost to the modern
masculine and technological consciousness. The tall shepherd of this

---

[50]  From "Trying to Pray", *The Branch Will Not Break* (Middletown, Conn., 1963), 42.
[51]  James Wright, "Depressed by a Book of Bad Poetry, I Walk Toward an Unused
Pasture and Invite the Insects to Join Me", *The Branch Will Not Break*, 36.
[52]  *Myths & Texts*, 7.
[53]  From "Matthew VIII, 28 ff.", *Walking to Sleep* (New York, 1969), 48.
[54]  From "O Taste and See", *O Taste and See* (New York, 1964), 53.
[55]  From "Out West", *The Rescued Year* (New York, 1966), 40.

being-in-the-world is Williams. "So much depends", he tells modern man, "upon / a red wheel / barrow..."[56]

For Descartes nothing at all depended on red wheelbarrows. Almost singlehandedly he built "the dreary shed" of the isolated consciousness in which truth resides apart as a matter of the mind, a mental formulation, a concept: "There used to be gods in everything, and now they've gone"[57] is the P.S. after "Cogito, ergo sum." But they are coming back in these poets' intuitive and connatural "care for daily things".[58] There are other signs that truth is slowly but surely being redefined. Vatican II is one of those signs and the philosophy of existentialism is another. In his book, *What is Existentialism?*, William Barrett constructs a dialogue between Alfred North Whitehead and Martin Heidegger in which they discuss the trend of philosophy in the last hundred years. Even the fact of their dialogue is significant; the form argues for the theme. The trend they agree to is: The Search for the Concrete. And that is also the trend, I believe, of contemporary American poetry. It is no accident that Sartre and Marcel write plays, that Heidegger is studying nineteenth-century German Romantic poetry. Truth is a matter of the whole person living his life at this time and in these circumstances, and it is not a matter of eternal mind. We hear the words 'anxiety' and 'care' and 'death' in connection with Heidegger, and though he is concerned with these he is more concerned with truth; that is the real focus of his attention. His two pamphlets, *Plato's Theory of Truth* and *On the Nature of Truth*, and the two books *Being and Time* and *Poetry, Language, Thought* argue that what we consider truth to be now, a matter of the mind, was not always the case, that actually our idea of truth is an aberration that begins with Plato from what the Greeks previously thought truth to consist in. His study takes note of the etymology of the Greek word for truth: 'not to escape notice'. The Greeks before Plato, Heidegger maintains, thought of truth as a matter of being: what is reveals itself and that revelation is truth. When things got detached from this ground for purposes of consideration, the nature of truth as well shifted from things in the whole context of their existence to the human mind judging correctly. It is my purpose here to show that contemporary poetry, particularly that of Gary Snyder, William Stafford, Richard Wilbur, and Howard Nemerov

---

[56] *Imaginations* (New York, 1970), 138.
[57] From "The Companions", Howard Nemerov, *The Blue Swallows* (Chicago, 1967), 19.
[58] From "Vermeer", Howard Nemerov, *The Next Room of the Dream* (Chicago, 1962), 37.

is concerned also with letting things be, with letting things reveal themselves; that their poetry marks a significant change in the history of
literature that is part of a larger and Romantic shift in Western culture
generally.

Perhaps it is appropriate to start in the middle of things. Here is an
extreme but not too atypical example of the new poetry from Gary
Snyder's *Myths & Texts:*

> Now I'll also tell what food
> we lived on then:
>
> Mescal, yucca fruit, pinyon, acorns,
> prickly pear, sumac berry, cactus,
> spurge, dropseed, lip fern, corn,
> mountain plants, wild potatoes, mesquite,
> stems of yucca, tree-yucca flowers, chokecherries,
> pitahaya cactus, honey of the ground-bee,
> honey, honey of the bumblebee,
> mulberries, angle-pod, salt, berries,
> berries of the one-seeded juniper,
> berries of the alligator-bark juniper,
> wild cattle, mule deer, antelopes,
> white-tailed deer, wild turkeys, doves, quail...[59]

As Henry James was fond of writing: "So there you are." One senses an
almost impish glee about the lines: Explicate me! More than the music of
the construction is of interest, though that is splendid indeed. No doubt
in the tradition of Williams, Snyder's is a presentation of things as things
with no meaning attached, with no irritable reaching for explanation and
extra significance beyond the fact that these things are. Thirty blows, the
Zen master says, whether you affirm or negate. Zen of course has always
been important to Snyder and for this reason, a reason that Carl Jung
underscores in his psychology: for Oriental man, to be locked up in
intellect is to be locked out of truth. This is not so much anti-intellectual-
ism as it is pro-being. In the East, what happened in Plato did not occur;
there was no detachment and therefore truth remained the revelation of
being. What D. T. Suzuki remarks of the spirit of Zen is the spirit of the
poem: "For here is no negation, no affirmation, but a plain fact, a pure
experience, the very foundation of our being and thought."[60] The highly

[59]   Pp. 28-29.
[60]   *An Introduction to Zen Buddhism* (New York, 1964), 51. Cf. Ernst Cassirer,
*Language and Myth*, 57. in the realm of mythic conception "nothing has any signifi-

heralded influence of Zen on contemporary poetry is no more, but no less, than an emphasis on truth as truth is being revealing itself. It is not so much that Snyder finds in Zen what he was looking for, but that he sees in it what he had already found in himself; the Japanese *Manyoshu* and Snyder's *Riprap, & Cold Mountain Poems* are parallel.[61] The search for the concrete cuts across many apparently diverse fields, and Zen is one of them, but certainly not the only one or even the main one. The climate of the time has asserted itself in all ways. It is significant, however, that we look to other cultures for an explanation of the emphasis on "the sheer fact of being alive".[62] From Plato forward, the concrete view seems foreign to us. Perplexed, critics speak of the Oriental ideas in Whitman, and similarly in Snyder. They are really minimal. The question is one of a quite native counteraction.

Very often the mind itself, nervous to make things mental, to misplace

---

cance or being save what is given in tangible reality. Here is no 'reference' and 'meaning'; every content of consciousness to which the mind is directed is immediately translated into terms of actual presence and effectiveness. Here thought does not confront its data in an attitude of free contemplation, seeking to understand their structure and their systematic connections, and analyzing them according to their parts and functions, but is simply captivated by a total impression. Such thinking does not develop the given content of experience; it does not reach backward or forward from that vantage point to find 'causes' and 'effects,' but rests content with taking in the sheer existent." Paul de Man discerns a similar captivation in Romanticism: "Ce changement se manifeste par un retour au concret, un foisonnement d'objets naturels et terrestres ramenant dans le langage la substantialité matérielle qui l'avait abandonné durant les siècles précédents" ("Structure intentionnelle de L'Image romantique", *Revue internationale de Philosophie*, XIV [1960], 68). One recalls particularly Keats's emphasis on negative capability and Wordsworth's injunction to wise passiveness in "Expostulation and Reply" as well as his invitation – an historic one in hindsight – in "The Tables Turned": "Come forth into the light of things..."

[61] Selected lyrics from the *Manyoshu*, with interpretive paintings by Sanko Inoue, have appeared as *Land of the Reed Plains* (Rutland, Vermont, 1960). Here are two lyrics that can be set beside Snyder's work:

On eastern meadows
glows the rosy tint of dawn
with a faint, soft gleam;
and as I glance behind me
there the moon is sinking low.

The rushing rapids
of the mountain river roar,
while across the peak
of lofty Mt. Yutsuki
the clouds ascend and hover.

[62] Gary Snyder, *Earth House Hold* (New York, 1969), 118.

concreteness, fidgety until the world can be intellectualized, philosophized, made four-square and simple and safe, is itself the subject of the poems. An example of this is Snyder's poem "Piute Creek":

> Words and books
> Like a small creek off a high ledge
> Gone in the dry air.
>
> A clear, attentive mind
> Has no meaning but that
> Which sees is truly seen.[63]

It might sound odd, but another way to come at this trend, to understand it a little better, is to think of Henry James. Actually he is very much like Gary Snyder; that does sound odd but it is true, true in the exact sense that truth for both of them is very much the same thing. Lambert Strether of *The Ambassadors* is the ambassador of the truth of being. That remarkable pilgrim's progress is to reverse the forward and upward trek we customarily value. He comes down to "the empire of 'things'". We see him seeing and therefore gradually turning away from judgment with relief in release to the real "smash" – "their walk, their déjeuner, their omelette, the Chablis, the place, the view, their present talk and his present pleasure in it..." What begins as statement in James turns finally to picture, to plain fact. His literature – and this argues his theme too – becomes as impressionistic as the world Strether stipples. What is enough for Gary Snyder is finally enough for Lambert Strether: "'Oh I don't think anything now!' Strether impatiently broke in: 'that is but what I *do* think!'"[64] Both James, and here Snyder, undo Plato:

> One granite ridge
> A tree, would be enough
> Or even a rock, a small creek,
> A bark-shred in a pool.

("Piute Creek")

Snyder's poem "Milton by Firelight" includes a vision of hell that a changed Strether would understand: an absence of daily event and sensuous detail. In the first two stanzas the poet questions the use of Milton's story of the Fall to his own labor on the mountain trails. Against it he urges switchbacks well made and the certainty of specific detail:

---

[63] *Riprap, & Cold Mountain Poems* (San Francisco, 1969), 6. Subsequent poems quoted are from this book.
[64] New York, 1909: I, 119; II, 15; I, 281.

Sleeping in saddle-blankets
Under a bright night-sky
Han River slantwise by morning
Jays squall
Coffee boils.

But such notation by firelight does lead him to discover the relevance of
Milton in a modern context. The third stanza projects a nightmarish
landscape of sterility that is linked with the mind and contrasted with
the full life of the two previous stanzas:

No paradise, no fall,
Only the weathering land
The wheeling sky,
Man, with his Satan
Scouring the chaos of the mind.
Oh Hell!

The final words also form an expletive that indicates the poet's own
growing impatience with these thoughts and with the fact that his campfire is going out. The final stanza quietly returns to the present and
partially negates the poet's own musing which now seems also general,
unimportant, and slightly foolish or pompous compared with the moment
around the campfire and the sounds of the moment that started such
revery in the first place:

Fire down
Too dark to read, miles from a road
The bell-mare clangs in the meadow
That packed dirt for a fill-in
Scrambling through loose rocks
On an old trail
All of a summer's day.

Yet the revery did yield dividends. To quote Frost, "The fact is the
sweetest dream that labor knows."[65]

What emerges from the poetry of Snyder is a sense of joy in the basic
recalcitrance of things to spiritualization. He eschews system and forecast
in letting things be. He knows full well that they will not, with emphasis,
by anything else. "The heart winces", as Wilbur wrote, "For junk and
gimcrack, / for jerrybuilt things";[66] that wince for things governs contemporary American poetry and establishes it as a poetry of being. It is
hard to imagine how Robert Francis could have written "Squash in

[65]   From "Mowing", *Complete Poems*, 25.
[66]   From "Junk", *The Poems of Richard Wilbur* (New York, 1963), 10.

Blossom" ("How lush, how loose, the uninhibited squash is"), "Tomatoes"
("Their hot vermilion luster, / Their unassailable three-dimensionality"),
"Waxwings", "Apple Peeler", or "Sailboat, Your Secret" in any other
climate.[67]

Like Gary Snyder, William Stafford is a poet of the Northwest. The
valleys and rivers of Oregon make up the landscape of his poetry as the
mountains and lakes of northwestern Washington figure in Snyder's.
The job he sets for himself is the one his father tells him in the poem
"Vocation", from the volume *Traveling through the Dark:* "Your job
is to find what the world is trying to be." What the world is trying to be
we discover in the poem "In Dear Detail, by Ideal Light":

> an imagined place
>
> Where finally the way the world feels
> really means how things are,
> in dear detail,
> by ideal light all around us.[68]

The poet's imagining takes the form of helping the world along in the
dream it is having about itself. For Stafford nature is the imagined place
from which nurture or civilization is a falling off and a detachment.
Only in nature for Stafford does dear detail and ideal light harmonize.
An example of this is the poem "At Cove on the Crooked River". This is
the second stanza:

> And the river there meant something
> always coming from snow and flashing around boulders
> after shadow-fish lurking below the mesa.

But what the river meant will not be known by the mind alone. It does
come from snow above but it also includes in its course the lurking
shadow-fish below. Put in psychological terms – geography is often close
to psychology in Stafford – its course mediates the conscious and the
unconscious mind. Furthermore, it is nature that is most like art; it is
the model of Stafford's poetry:

> Oh civilization, I want to carve you like this,
> decisively outward the way evening comes
> over that kind of twist in the scenery
>
> When people cramp into their station wagons
> and roll up the windows, and drive away.

---

[67]  *The Orb Weaver* (Middletown, Conn., 1960).
[68]  New York, 1962, 92. Subsequent poems quoted are from this book.

These lines indicate the pastoral strain of Stafford's poetry that makes
him part of a larger tradition in American literature. As so often in
Thoreau, Twain, Hemingway, and Faulkner, here too a vision of simplicity is brought into context with the nonsimple that it measures and finds
wanting. The decisive frankness and openness of nature, carefully ordered,
is offset by a close and cluttered, deceptive and introspective nurture.
Driving off is a detachment from this free and open but ordered and
therefore whole experience. Robert Bly and James Wright share this
pastoral mode.

In the poem "Representing Far Places", again Stafford notices the
discrepancy between nature and nurture, this time witty society and the
canoe wilderness:

> In the canoe wilderness branches wait for winter;
> every leaf concentrates; a drop from the paddle falls.
> Up through water at the dip of a falling leaf
> to the sky's drop of light or the smell of another star
> fish in the lake leap arcs of realization,
> hard fins prying out from the dark below.
>
> Often in society when the talk turns witty
> you think of that place, and can't polarize at all:
> it would be a kind of treason. The land fans in your head
> canyon by canyon; steep roads diverge.
> Representing far places you stand in the room,
> all that you know merely a weight in the weather.
>
> It is all right to be simply the way you have to be,
> among contradictory ridges in some crescendo of knowing.

The fact of being eludes judgment. The poet will not even pretend that he
can leap from the fact to any significance; it is too rich for wit; its background too full in the arcs of realization between the sky's light and the
dark below. Knowledge is brought up short, or transcends itself, among
contradictory ridges. The theme, while it recalls the psychological geography of "At Cove on the Crooked River", is like that in the poem
"Returned to Say" where the poet contrasts the life of a Cree Indian with
our own: "We will mean what he does."

Richard Wilbur is just as happy in the full dimensionality of the world.
It is no springboard for him either; he relishes all its contours. One of
his poems is titled, after Traherne, "A World Without Objects Is a
Sensible Emptiness".[69] Like Stafford, he wins us in this poem to dear

---

[69]  *The Poems of Richard Wilbur*, 117. Subsequent poems quoted are from this book.

detail; only here can ideal light be found. The ideal is the real for Wilbur, as it was for Coleridge. If Coleridge was right about a symbol being the translucence of the eternal through and in the temporal, then this poem is a symbol and contemporary American poetry is symbolic. Wilbur hangs on for dear life, and ours, to the temporal. The poem dramatizes the inadequacy of modern man's idea of truth as that misconception grows out of another – his idea of God as transcendent. Wilbur urges the Nativity upon us. Insight can only come from a plunge into the concrete. In the first four stanzas the "tall camels of the spirit", modern magi, "Steer for their deserts", but in the last three stanzas the poet directs these "connoisseurs of thirst" elsewhere:

> Turn, O turn
> From the fine sleights of the sand, from the long empty oven
> Where flames in flamings burn
> Back to the trees arrayed
> In bursts of glare, to the halo-dialing run
> Of the country creeks, and the hills' bracken tiaras made
> Gold in the sunken sun,
>
> Wisely watch for the sight
> Of the supernova burgeoning over the barn,
> Lampshine blurred in the steam of beasts, the spirit's right
> Oasis, light incarnate.

Sanctity is not a matter of otherworldliness; the poet anchors it in this world with a decisively powerful particularity. Wilbur advises himself in the poem to remember the early painters who capped the saints with merry-go-round rings (not halos) "jauntily worn". The advise is his own aesthetic, close to that of Coleridge and Browning. The parallel reminds us of the Romantic heritage of contemporary poetry, Romantic insofar as that term is associated with Coleridge's definition of the imagination that reveals itself in the balance or reconciliation of the idea with the image, the general and abstract with the particular and concrete. That is the advice Wilbur gives the camels of the spirit when he directs them to the material. Christ, who reconciles heaven and earth, can be found where the idea is made flesh, where the star shines over the barn in the poem. Thus his own works, Wilbur wrote in *Shenandoah*, "incline... to favor a spirituality which is not abstracted, not dissociated and world-renouncing".[70] Edgar Degas' unique gesture in the poem "Museum

---

[70]  "On My Own Work", XVII (1965), 66.

Piece" defines Wilbur's own view and aesthetic: Degas used a painting of El Greco "to hang his pants on while he slept".

William Whitla notices a similar connection between religious reconciliation and creative purpose in his book *The Central Truth: The Incarnation in Browning's Poetry*. We can see now that Browning, and Victorian poetry for that matter, does not break from Romantic poetry but continues it and bolsters it. Through Browning, Romanticism comes to Pound and Eliot and through them and Williams to Wilbur, to Nemerov, Stafford and Snyder. To put it simply, the line of evolution is toward a pure and purer conjunction until the idea can not be divided from the image. Just as the Incarnation is used by Browning (especially in "Fra Lippo Lippi" and in "Saul") and Eliot (in *Four Quartets*, especially "Dry Salvages") as the foundation of their themes, so Wilbur has used the Nativity in "A World Without Objects Is a Sensible Emptiness". And all three apply their larger themes to art itself. Browning often used painters and musicians to give his poems this aesthetic dimension; Eliot continually asks in his poems whether the words used have been adequate to convey the Word; and Wilbur does both. Art should be whole, make manifest what it is about (Heidegger's definition of truth); art too should incarnate. What Ralph Mills noted of Wilbur's poem "October Maples, Portland" is true of his work generally: the natural world "is changed in the poet's eye, and through his deft use of analogy and allusion, into a sacramental reality: the zones of the spiritual and the material draw together momentarily in the poem, there to be experienced again and again".[71] That is what the poem is about and that is what the poem does: shows the eternal through and in the temporal. In the poem "A Prayer to Go to Paradise with the Donkeys", Francis Jammes imagines a heaven that is much like his own life on earth but in a finer tone. He would be lost without his donkeys and their "loads of feather-dusters and kitchenwares". Like the painting of the Madonna and Child Fra Lippo intends, the pleasures of time are set in timelessness:

> Dear God, let it be with these donkeys that I come,
> And let it be that angels lead us in peace
> To leafy streams where cherries tremble in air,
> Sleek as the laughing flesh of girls...

Francis Jammes can only think in images and that is precisely the point. His imagining is closest to the fact of the Incarnation – the same fact George Santayana overlooked in Browning's poetry when he called its

[71] *Contemporary American Poetry* (New York, 1966), 169.

sensual heavens barbaric.[72] Wilbur also catches us up in irony if we admire the vision of Francis Jammes as touching or pleasant and poignant. Another phrase to describe contemporary American poetry, instead of a poetry of being, might be a poetry of the secular as sacred.

From the beginning Wilbur's poetry has had a religious intent that at first glance might not seem religious at all because we are not accustomed to thinking of religion in terms of the eternal-temporal. Santayana is an example. But religion implies a bond between God and time and Wilbur chooses to emphasize in that bond all that is involved in time: country creeks, kitchen-wares, junk, mountain fern, merry-go-rounds, everything. Having become man, it is in man and in time that Christ is to be found. He is a very religious poet in this sense. These lines are from his poem "Advice to a Prophet":

> Speak of the world's own change. Though we cannot conceive
> Of an undreamt thing, we know to our cost
> How the dreamt cloud crumbles, the vines are blackened by frost,
> How the view alters.

It is advice the poet must follow as well. The prophet's rhetoric, or the poet's, can itself be the stuff of prophecy. "A Christmas Hymn" celebrates the cardinal fact of history for Wilbur. The words, shifting between opposites, partake of the reality they render:

> But now, as at the ending,
> The low is lifted high;
> The stars shall bend their voices,
> And every stone shall cry.
> And every stone shall cry
> In praises of the child
> By whose descent among us
> The worlds are reconciled.

Stafford is content with natural imagery – the leap of fish between sky and water, the arcs of realization. Wilbur is too, but here he uncovers the strong foundation of the new approach. His poetry in theme and technique more and more rests upon truth as this hypostasis "Where word with world is one / And Nothing dies" ("Games Two"), rather than concept or judgment or proposition.

As Eliot says in the preface to his translation of St.-John Perse, "there is a logic of the imagination as well as a logic of concepts";[73] it is the

---

[72]  Chapter VII "The Poetry of Barbarism", *Interpretations of Poetry and Religion.*
[73]  *Anabasis* (New York, 1949), 10.

logic of the imagination that Heidegger and contemporary poets find true. Heidegger would recognize poetic perceptions of his own insight in Wilbur's work. "Attention Makes Infinity" is an obvious example but there are many others, such as "Love Calls Us to the Things of This World", or here, "A Problem from Milton":

> Poor Adam, deviled by your energy,
> What power egged you on to feed your brains?
> Envy the gorgeous gallops of the sea,
> Whose horses never know their lunar reins.

or "La Rose des Vents":

> Forsake those roses
> Of the mind
> And tend the true,
> The mortal flower.

and certainly "Epistemology":

> We milk the cow of the world, and as we do
> We whisper in her ear, "you are not true."

Someone remarked of Wordsworth that he combines John Locke and St. Francis. Whether we can substitute Martin Heidegger for Locke in an estimation of Wilbur, or not, still what is true in Wordsworth is true in Wilbur: "We see into the life of things."

Howard Nemerov has a more satiric voice than Wilbur, especially in *The Next Room of the Dream*, but the direction in *New and Selected Poems* (1960) and *The Blue Swallows* (1967) does strongly remind us of Wilbur, especially in what James Dickey, in *The Suspect in Poetry*, has noted in Nemerov as "the casual-serious meditation from nature, in which the schooled modern intelligence looks through or past its burden of knowledge into the brute Fact of an aspect of the surrounding world".[74] This criticism is a little deceptive, however. Knowledge is not repudiated on behalf of the concrete. It defines the pull of the concrete through its own distance from the concrete. The marriage of thoughts and things is by poetic proxy; through remembrance the poet both maintains and eliminates the mind's distance from the world:

> It's taken that long for the mind
> To waken, yawn and stretch, to see
> With opened eyes emptied of speech

[74] Madison, Minn., 1964, 62.

> The real world where the spelling mind
> Imposes with its grammar book
> Unreal relations on the blue
> Swallows.
>
> . . . . . . . . . . . . . .
>
> O swallows, swallows, poems are not
> The point. Finding again the world,
> That is the point, where loveliness
> Adorns intelligible things
> Because the mind's eye lit the sun.[75]

("The Blue Swallows")

Like Wilbur this point becomes in Nemerov the poem itself, the work
of art that mediates man and nature and counteracts the divisive tendency
of the mind. The poem "Writing" is an example of this. The poet notices
that letters themselves have a delight all their own. Chinese characters
remind him of skaters "scoring their white / records on ice":

> Being intelligible,
> these winding ways with their audacities
> and delicate hesitations, they become
> miraculous, so intimately, out there
> at the pen's point or brush's tip, do world
> and spirit wed.[76]

That, I think, is about the best explanation we shall ever have for Pound's
interest in the Chinese character. For him too it wedded image with
idea. Nemerov sees this as the nature of art, the specific function of the
artist and of the poet in particular. The search for the concrete in him
is a search for such synthesis in which the poet gingerly steers his way
between the idea and the fact, carefully fusing them:

> The way a word does when
> It senses on one side
> A thing and on the other
> A thought; at either side
> It glances and goes deep
> Together;
>
> . . . . . . . . . . .
>
> That is one way of doing
> One's being in a world

---

[75] *The Blue Swallows*, 89-90.
[76] *New and Selected Poems* (Chicago, 1963), 75. Unless otherwise noted, subsequent
poems quoted are from this book.

Whose being is both thought
And thing, where neither thing
Nor thought will do alone
Till either answers other;
Two lovers in the night
Each sighing other's name
Whose alien syllables
Become synonymous...[77]

("One Way")

Nemerov also draws a parallel for the one way – it is more than a parallel –
with the Incarnation. There is a definite relationship in this respect
between the poems "Painting a Mountain Stream" and "To Lu Chi" with
"Carol". The first two are about art (painting and poetry) and the third
about the birth of Christ. The point is that they become almost convertible.
In "Carol" he could as well be writing about poetry and in "To Lu Chi"
about Christ's birth. "Painting a Mountain Stream" begins with lines
any Church Father would have been proud of:

Running and standing still at once
is the whole truth.

One thinks of St. Ambrose and St. Augustine at their best. But at this
point Nemerov is writing about art. The sixth stanza reads:

In the confluence of the wrist
things and ideas ripple together,
as in the clear lake of the eye,
unfathomably, running remains.

The poem "To Lu Chi" carries this one step further. Nemerov tells
us that Lu Chi was the author of *Wen Fu, or Prose Poem on the Art of
Letters* (A.D. 302). Whatever the poem tells us about Lu Chi's aesthetic,
it also tells us about Howard Nemerov's; it is quite clearly his own. The
poem is a casual-serious meditation on art, an apology for it in a world
of active and contemplative men who have little use for art, a world in
other words just about like the world at any time, like Lu Chi's, or
Pound's in "Hugh Selwyn Mauberly" which the poem recalls in a
number of lines. To the active man and to the contemplative man the
poet can say nothing directly. He must proceed by rich indirection like
Lu Chi just before dawn, with his robes tucked in his belt, "Fishing that

[77] *The Blue Swallows*, 86.

stream" where things and ideas ripple together in the larger and saving
truth of whole experience:

> But look into the clear and mirroring stream
> Where images remain although the water
> Passes away. Neither action nor thought,
> Only the concentration of our speech
> In fineness and in strength (your axe again),
> Till it can carry, in those other minds,
> A nobler action and a purer thought.

Here too, as he says of Lu Chi's work, "the art of letters turns / To the
inspection of itself". The search is for the mastery of writing "Where
the heron fishes in his own image", where the poet's description and the
actual deed itself begin to intermingle. If the lines from "Writing" clarify
Pound's interest in Chinese, these certainly remind us of Eliot's images in
"Burnt Norton" of the still point "Neither flesh nor fleshless" and the
Chinese jar that "Moves perpetually in its stillness". As I have suggested,
Eliot uses the Incarnation to point the way for an answer to this paradoxi-
cal desire of man that he expressed in the still point and the Chinese jar.
And Nemerov, like Eliot, makes this desire and this answer reverberate
back on his function as a poet using words and trying to make them be
what they mean, trying to make the words flesh. The last lines of "To
Lu Chi" indicate this direction:

> I shall pretend to be a poet all
> This afternoon, a Chinese poet, and
> My marvelous words must bring the springtime in
> And the great tree of speech to flower
> Between the two realms of heaven and earth.

The poet's "marvelous" words (recall "miraculous" in the poem "Writing") become directly related to the Word being made Flesh in "Carol".
The language is almost the same, as we might expect:

> For there was born at Bethlehem
> *In silence and night*
> The world's and heaven's single stem
> That to both kingdoms we might then
> Say Amen.

The image of the tree is common to both poems. It describes what the
poet does in "To Lu Chi" and we find in the poem "Carol" through the
same image that what he does is similar to what Christ is. It should be
clear now how contemporary poets can turn to the East and yet sound
more and more Christian. They have found a substratum between the

two that happens to be the religious counterpart of their own aesthetic endeavor, a counterpart that indeed more often than not touches the fact of literature as similar to itself.[78] Both the East and the West say Amen (Aum in the East) to both kingdoms, kingdoms too that the poet would have his poem be the single stem between. If the world and man are to be brought together it seems that the East and the West are to be too.

When East meets West, Owen Barfield remarked, the spirit of romance is born. In any case the spirit of Romanticism lingers on in these contemporary poets and certainly in Nemerov. His emphasis on trees alone, a rather constant Romantic metaphor, is enough to cement this. But trees for Nemerov, as for Coleridge, are rather more than justifications for organic form. Nemerov does of course stress the vital and the dynamic, as most contemporary poets do as a kind of feedback to the modern mechanization of life (Nemerov's poem "A Singular Metamorphosis" is a good example of this: where there are TV sets let us sow trees), but there is another more primary reason for the frequency of trees and the related imagery of trees in Nemerov's poetry. Here is one of his best poems:

> To be a giant and keep quiet about it,
> To stay in one's own place;
> To stand for the constant presence of process
> And always to seem the same;
> To be steady as a rock and always trembling,
> Having the hard appearance of death
> With the soft, fluent nature of growth,
> One's Being deceptively armored,
> One's Becoming deceptively vulnerable;
> To be so tough, and take the light so well,
> Freely providing forbidden knowledge
> Of so many things about heaven and earth
> For which we should otherwise have no word –
> Poems or people are rarely so lovely,
> And even when they have great qualities
> They tend to tell you rather than exemplify
> What they believe themselves to be about,
> While from the moving silence of trees,

[78] Cf. Nemerov's essay "The Swaying Form: A Problem in Poetry", in *Poetry and Fiction* (New Brunswick, N. J., 1963), 13: "The relation of poetry to religion is both intimate and antithetical, for poetry exists only by a continuing revelation in a world always incarnate of word and flesh indissolubly, a world simultaneously solid and transpicuous... Poetry and institutionalized religion are in a sense the flowing and the static forms of the same substance, liquid and solid states of the same elemental energy."

> Whether in storm or calm, in leaf and naked,
> Night or day, we draw conclusions of our own,
> Sustaining and unnoticed as our breath,
> And perilous also – though there has never been
> A critical tree – about the nature of things.

("Trees")

The first thing to notice is that they exemplify what they are about. Heidegger defined truth in almost the same words: it lets us see something from the very thing it is about *(von dem selbst her, wovon die Rede ist).*[79] The tree lets us see exactly what it is – the same yet different, steady but trembling, deathlike and alive, a being becoming. The mind is brought up short again, or transcends itself, among these contradictory attributes. Only the imagination is at home here. What the tree does and what the poet imagines coincide. The imagination has nothing to do with fantasy whatsoever. Probably as a result of the change in the definition of truth, however, this faculty, the faculty most associated with the true from the beginning, was relegated to a very secondary position, even to the point that what is imaginary is thought to be untrue. What Plato thought of poets followed logically from his shift out of being into consideration. In this way the intellect secured its ground; it debunked the imagination in defense of its own usurpation. What is most truthful is not even thought to be truthful at all, but indeed false – at best just pleasant, a sort of diversion or holiday. But this defense – one of the most momentous for Western culture – was questioned by Coleridge. Coleridge reasserted the imagination – equally momentous for Western culture. And if the imagination reveals itself in the balance or reconciliation of opposite qualities, so does the tree. Our desire to draw conclusions about trees even defines what makes us want to do that: trees do not; they are.

Fascination with trees is not peculiar to Nemerov among contemporary poets. One thinks of the first stanza of Robert Bly's "Hunting Pheasants in a Cornfield" from *Silence in the Snowy Fields:*

> What is so strange about a tree alone in an open field?
> It is a willow tree. I walk around and around it.
> The body is strangely torn, and cannot leave it.
> At last I sit down beneath it.[80]

Still, Nemerov develops the relationship in what trees exemplify and poems do with what Christ is. The fifteen "Runes" that develop this triple

---

[79]  *Being and Time,* 56.
[80]  Middletown, Conn., 1964, 14.

relationship of the natural, the aesthetic, and the religious are Nemerov's *Four Quartets*. The paradoxical language, like Eliot's, is part of the theme again; the mind by itself must be stymied and shut off to be made ready for truth, the revelation of being. The first rune begins with the line "This is about the stillness in moving things", and continues:

> That is my theme, of thought and the defeat
> Of thought before its object, where it turns
> As from a mirror, and returns to be
> The thought of something and the thought of thought,
> A trader doubly burdened, commercing
> Out of one stillness and into another.

Rune four begins the countermovement after the defeat of thought. Here the poet's craft, the tree, and Christ begin to intermingle in very complex ways:

> For each stone bears the living word, each word
> Will be made flesh, and all flesh fall to seed:
> Such stones from the tree; and from the stones, such blood.

Rune five develops the slowly burgeoning theme of Christ's sacrifice that is interlocked with the poet's atonement in his imagining for the detachment of knowledge from being; he too reconciles when he makes ideas flesh:

> The fat time of the year is also time
> Of the Atonement; birds to the berry bushes,
> Men to the harvest...

In rune eleven the poet reflects upon the atonement that has already occurred. On the religious level the world has been rejoined to heaven. On the literary level the holy man advises the poet to look for the infinite in the finite. The poet reveals a return to the concrete as synthesis by splitting the stick and finding that it is both wood and God: "I saw nothing that was not wood, nothing / That was not God." This is followed by a dream of the tree "whereon the Son of Man / Hung between thieves". Rune fifteen urges upon the reader what the poet has discovered naturally, aesthetically, and religiously. Human beings must reach a similar totality: they must redirect the mind to nature, imagine, and be Christlike in order to be complete and happy:

> To watch water, to watch running water
> Is to know a secret, seeing the twisted rope
> Of runnels on the hillside, the small freshets
> Leaping and limping down the tilted field

In April's light, the green, grave and opaque
Swirl in the millpond where the current slides
To be combed and carded silver at the fall;
It is a secret. Or it is not to know
The secret, but to have it in your keeping,
A locked box, Bluebeard's room, the deathless thing
Which it is death to open. Knowing the secret,
Keeping the secret – herringbones of light
Ebbing on beaches, the huge artillery
Of tides – it is not knowing, it is not keeping,
But being the secret hidden from yourself.

Alfred North Whitehead remarked that all history is a series of footnotes to Plato. To the extent that there are two-Platos-in-one, this is particularly true of the Romantic movement which reacts negatively in Keats to the rationalistic Plato who would divide Being, and positively in Emerson to the imaginative Plato who would include meaning and manifestation in his definition of Being and all. The ultimate reach of his thought in God turned him back to the world, and it is between these two movements that history swings until Romanticism right up to and including the present moment took its stand between them at a third point whose basic message is individualized by each writer: Give us both: "Beauty is truth, truth beauty." And what all these writers imagine is true.

# SELECTIVE BIBLIOGRAPHY

Abrams, M. H., *Natural Supernaturalism: Tradition and Revolution in Romantic Literature* (New York: W. W. Norton, 1971).

Balakian, Anna, *Surrealism: the Road to the Absolute* (New York: Noonday, 1959).

Barrett, William, *Irrational Man: A Study in Existential Philosophy* (Garden City, New York: Doubleday Anchor, 1962).

Benziger, James, *Images of Eternity: Studies in the Poetry of Religious Vision from Wordsworth to T. S. Eliot* (Carbondale, Illinois: Southern Illinois University Press, 1964).

Berdyaev, Nicolas, *The Beginning and the End*, trans. R. M. French (New York: Harper & Row, 1957).

—, *The Meaning of History*, trans. George Reavey (Cleveland: World Publishing Company, 1962).

Campbell, Joseph, *The Hero with a Thousand Faces* (Cleveland: World Publishing Company, 1964).

Cassirer, Ernst, *Language and Myth*, trans. Susanne K. Langer (Harper & Brothers, 1946; rpt. New York: Dover, 1953).

Coleridge, Samuel Taylor, *The Complete Works of Samuel Taylor Coleridge*, ed. W. G. T. Shedd, 7 vols. (New York: Harper & Brothers, 1863-1865).

—, *Biographia Literaria*, ed. J. Shawcross, 2 vols. (Clarendon Press, 1907; rpt. London: Oxford University Press, 1958).

—, *The Complete Poetical Works of Samuel Taylor Coleridge*, ed. Ernest Hartley Coleridge, 2 vols. (Clarendon Press, 1912; rpt. Oxford: The University Press, 1957).

Deutschbein, Max, *Das Wesen des Romantischen* (Cöthen: Schulze, 1921).

Drew, Elizabeth, *T. S. Eliot: The Design of His Poetry* (New York: Charles Scribner's Sons, 1949).

Eliade, Mircea, *Patterns in Comparative Religion: A Study of the Element of the Sacred in the History of Religious Phenomena*, trans. Rosemary Sheed (Cleveland: World Publishing Company, 1963).

—, *Mephistopheles and the Androgyne: Studies in Religious Myth and Symbol*, trans. J. M. Cohen (New York: Sheed and Ward, 1965).

Eliot, T. S., *Collected Poems 1909-1962* (New York: Harcourt Brace & World, 1963).

—, *Selected Essays* (New York: Harcourt Brace, 1950).

Emerson, Ralph Waldo, *The Complete Works of Ralph Waldo Emerson*, ed. Edward Waldo Emerson, 12 vols. (Boston: Houghton Mifflin, 1903-1921).

—, *Journals of Ralph Waldo Emerson*, eds. Edward Waldo Emerson and Waldo Emerson Forbes, 10 vols. (Boston: Houghton Mifflin, 1909-1914).

—, *The Complete Essays and Other Writings of Ralph Waldo Emerson*, ed. Brooks Atkinson (New York: Modern Library, 1950).

Fausset, Hugh, *The Proving of Psyche* (New York: Harcourt, 1929).

Feidelson, Charles, Jr., *Symbolism and American Literature* (Chicago: University of Chicago Press, 1959).

Gérard, Albert S., "On the Logic of Romanticism", *Criticism*, VII (1957), 262-273.

—, *English Romantic Poetry: Ethos, Structure, and Symbol in Coleridge, Wordsworth, Shelley, and Keats* (Berkeley: University of California Press, 1968).

Gray, Henry David, *Emerson: A Statement of New England Transcendentalism as Expressed in the Philosophy of Its Chief Exponent* (Stanford University Press, 1917; rpt. New York: Frederick Ungar, 1970).

Hawthorne, Nathaniel, *The Centenary Edition of the Works of Nathaniel Hawthorne*, ed. William Charvat, et al., 5 vols. (Columbus, Ohio: Ohio State University Press, 1962-1970).

—, *Great Short Works of Nathaniel Hawthorne*, ed. Frederick C. Crews (New York: Harper & Row, 1967).

Hegel, Georg W. F., *Hegel: Selections*, ed. Jacob Loewenberg (New York: Charles Scribner's Sons, 1957).

Heidegger, Martin, *An Introduction to Metaphysics*, trans. Ralph Manheim (Garden City, New York: Doubleday Anchor, 1961).

—, *Being and Time*, trans. John Macquarrie and Edward Robinson (New York: Harper & Row, 1962).

—, *Poetry, Language, Thought*, trans. Albert Hofstadter (New York: Harper & Row, 1971).

Jacobi, Jolande, *The Psychology of C. G. Jung*, trans. Ralph Manheim, 5th ed. (1951; rpt. New Haven, Connecticut: Yale University Press, 1964).

Jung, C. G., *Psyche and Symbol: A Selection from the Writings of C. G. Jung*, ed. Violet S. de Laszlo (Garden City, New York: Doubleday Anchor, 1958).

—, *Psychology and Religion* (New Haven, Connecticut: Yale University Press, 1964).

Jung, C. G., et al., *Man and His Symbols* (New York: Dell, 1971).

Keats, John, *The Letters of John Keats*, ed. Hyder Edward Rollins, 2 vols. (Cambridge, Massachusetts: Harvard University Press, 1958).

—, *The Poetical Works of John Keats*, ed. H. W. Garrod, 2nd ed. (Oxford: Clarendon Press, 1958).

Kierkegaard, Søren, *Fear and Trembling, The Sickness Unto Death*, trans. Walter Lowrie (Garden City, New York: Doubleday Anchor, 1954).

Knight, G. Wilson, *The Starlit Dome: Studies in the Poetry of Vision* (New York: Barnes & Noble, 1960).

Lawrence, D. H., *Studies in Classic American Literature* (New York: Viking Press, 1961).

Lovejoy, Arthur O., *The Revolt Against Dualism: An Inquiry Concerning the Existence of Ideas* (La Salle, Illinois: Open Court Publishing Company, 1955).

—, *The Great Chain of Being: A Study of the History of an Idea* (Cambridge, Massachusetts: Harvard University Press, 1957).

—, *Essays in the History of Ideas* (New York: G. P. Putnam's Sons, 1960).

—, *The Reason, the Understanding, and Time* (Baltimore: Johns Hopkins Press, 1961).

Lynch, William, *Christ and Apollo: The Dimensions of the Literary Imagination* (New York: New American Library, 1963).

Man, Paul de, "Structure intentionelle de L'Image romantique", *Revue internationale de Philosophie*, XIV (1960), 68-84.

Maritain, Jacques, *Creative Intuition in Art and Poetry* (New York: Meridian, 1958).

Mills, Ralph J., Jr., *Contemporary American Poetry* (New York: Random House, 1966).

Nemerov, Howard, *The Next Room of the Dream* (Chicago: University of Chicago Press, 1962).

—, *New & Selected Poems* (Chicago: University of Chicago Press, 1963).

—, *Poetry and Fiction: Essays* (New Brunswick, New Jersey: Rutgers University Press, 1963).

—, *The Blue Swallows* (Chicago: University of Chicago Press, 1967).

Neumann, Erich, *Art and the Creative Unconscious: Four Essays*, trans. Ralph Manheim (New York: Pantheon, 1959).

—, *The Archetypal World of Henry Moore*, trans. R. F. C. Hull (Pantheon, 1959; rpt. New York: Harper & Row, 1965).

—, *The Origins and History of Consciousness*, trans. R. F. C. Hull (New York: Pantheon, 1964).

Peckham, Morse, "Toward a Theory of Romanticism", *PMLA*, LXVI (1951), 5-23.

—, "Toward a Theory of Romanticism: II. Reconsiderations", *Studies in Romanticism*, I (1961), 1-8.

Poulet, Georges, "Timelessness and Romanticism", *Journal of the History of Ideas*, XV (1954), 3-22.

Read, Herbert, *The Philosophy of Modern Art* (New York: Horizon Press, 1953).

—, *The True Voice of Feeling: Studies in English Romantic Poetry* (New York: Pantheon, 1953).

*Romanticism: Points of View*, eds. Robert F. Gleckner and Gerald E. Enscoe, 2nd ed. (Englewood Cliffs, New Jersey: Prentice-Hall, 1970).

Schelling, Friedrich, *The Ages of the World*, trans. and ed. Frederick de Wolfe Bolman, Jr. (New York: Columbia University Press, 1942).

Scott, Nathan A., Jr., *The Broken Center: Studies in the Theological Horizon of Modern Literature* (New Haven: Yale University Press, 1968).

Snyder, Gary, *Myths & Texts* (New York: Totem Press, 1960).

—, *Earth House Hold: Technical Notes & Queries to Fellow Dharma Revolutionaries* (New York: New Directions, 1969).

—, *Riprap, & Cold Mountain Poems* (San Francisco: City Lights Books, 1969).

Stafford, William, *Traveling through the Dark* (New York: Harper & Row, 1962).

—, *The Rescued Year* (New York: Harper & Row, 1966).

Stern, Karl, *The Flight from Woman* (New York: Farrar, Straus and Giroux, 1965).

Suzuki, D. T., *An Introduction to Zen Buddhism*, Foreword by C. G. Jung (New York: Grove Press, 1964).

Teilhard de Chardin, Pierre, *The Future of Man*, trans. Norman Denny (New York: Harper & Row, 1964).

—, *Hymn of the Universe*, trans. Simon Bartholomew (New York: Harper & Row, 1965).

Thoreau, Henry David, *The Writings of Henry David Thoreau*, 20 vols. (Houghton Mifflin, 1906; rpt. New York: AMS Press, 1968).

Vivante, Leone, *English Poetry and Its Contribution to the Knowledge of a Creative Principle*, Preface by T. S. Eliot (Faber and Faber, 1950; rpt. Carbondale, Illinois: Southern Illinois University Press, 1963).

Wasserman, Earl R., *The Finer Tone: Keats' Major Poems* (Baltimore: Johns Hopkins Press, 1963).

White, Victor, *God and the Unconscious: An Encounter between Psychology and Religion* (Cleveland: World Publishing Company, 1961).

Whitman, Walt, *The Complete Writings of Walt Whitman*, eds. Richard Maurice Bucke, Thomas B. Harned, and Horace L. Traubel, 10 vols. (New York: G. P. Putnam's Sons, 1902).

Wilbur, Richard, *The Poems of Richard Wilbur* (New York: Harcourt Brace & World, 1963).

—, *Walking to Sleep: New Poems and Translations* (New York: Harcourt Brace & World, 1969).

Wilhelm, Hellmut, *Change: Eight Lectures on the "I Ching"*, trans. Cary F. Baynes (Pantheon, 1960; rpt. New York: Harper & Row, 1964).

Zimmer, Heinrich, *Myths and Symbols in Indian Art and Civilization*, ed. Joseph Campbell (Pantheon, 1946; rpt. New York: Harper & Row, 1962).

# INDEX